JESUS IS NOT REPUBLICAN

A SECULAR LIBERAL'S ADVENTURES WITH RELIGION, POLITICS AND SEX

KATE RICE

Copyright © 2021 by Kate Rice

All rights reserved.

No part of this book may be reproduced in any form or by any electronic or mechanical means, including information storage and retrieval systems, without written permission from the author, except for the use of brief quotations in a book review.

❀ Created with Vellum

To Jim Rice

Who Practiced Faith and Humor

CONTENTS

1. Glamping for Jesus	1
2. Hijacking Jesus	17
3. A Racist God	36
4. Trump the Messiah: Christian Nationalism	52
5. Jesus Is My Vaccine	68
6. True Love: Gay Christians	87
7. The Evangelical Exodus	103
8. If Sex Is So Bad, Why Did God Make It So Fun?	117
9. Montezuma County: Paradox and Parable	141
10. Progressive Christianity: Not An Oxymoron	183
11. Working the Margins With Jesus	199
12. Not The End	220
About the Author	229
Also by Kate Rice	231

1

GLAMPING FOR JESUS

It was a hot and sultry July afternoon deep in the Blue Ridge Mountains, where cellphone signals can't penetrate and sun-faded Confederate flags fly.

I was part of a sweating crowd listening to a preacher. We sat in a big white tent with the sides rolled up, the type of tent religious revivalists might use when they're crying out to the Lord to save us sinners from eternal hellfire.

But this preacher was very different from that stereotype. In fact, that stereotypical pastor probably would have tried to exorcise what he would consider the demons possessing the crowd I sat with. And he would have started with our preacher — one Nadia-Bolz Weber, all six feet of her, dramatic streaks of gray in her dark hair, and a big Mary Magdalene tattoo on a bicep muscular enough to make Michelle Obama jealous.

She is a Lutheran minister who says crazy things like sex is good. Even if you're not married, even if you're gay or trans or bi. A preacher who asks, "Isn't forgiving abusive men over and over what keeps battered women battered?" A minister whose congregants don't fit the cookie cutter that my Holy Roller preacher — and a lot of conservative Christians — would try to make us all fit into. No, her flock included straight, gay, trans, the newly sober, the-trying-to-be-sober, the eternally — and humanly — imperfect.

As she wound up her talk, the crowd stayed with her, cheering and clapping. And then she said, "C'mon up and dance with me!"

My new friend Jes, her asymmetrically cut hair swinging, a wicked glint in her eye, grabbed my hand and pulled a hesitant me out of my chair.

"Okay, Kate, let's go!" she said.

And we ran up to the stage together, joining dozens of others as the loudspeakers blasted Prince's *Kiss*. There I was dancing and singing, surprised at how many of the lyrics I knew by this artistic genius who transcended conventional boundaries of gender, sex and identity. It was the perfect soundtrack for this crowd, some straight, some gay, some transgender, some Christian, and some, like me, not Christian at all.

Whatever I had expected of a progressive Christian festival, this was definitely not it.

I had had no idea of what I'd be getting into when I'd left my triplex apartment on Manhattan's deep blue Upper West Side two days earlier. I'd taken an early morning flight out of LaGuardia to Atlanta, then boarded a zippy little Bombardier for the quick hop to the Asheville, North Carolina, airport where I picked up a rental car.

Driving out of Asheville, I wound north and west on US-25, my rented Chevy Spark's feeble but valiant engine laboring up the first hills leading into the Blue Ridge Mountains, That's when I lost my internet connection for the bulk of the weekend. My route took me through a green-as-a-tropical-jungle landscape, occasionally passing a weather-beaten house with a tattered Confederate flag rippling in a hot breeze.

C'mon, man, I thought, having internal monologues with the owners of homes flying those flags. *It's been more than 150 years! You lost!* Then I realized we're still fighting that battle. And I was headed toward a very different rebel enclave, one that fights against all that that flag stands for.

My destination: Hot Springs, North Carolina., so named for the 100-degree-plus mineral springs that have attracted people for centuries. It's a small town that's a handful of one- and two-story buildings on one side of a railroad track. On the other side, the Hot Springs Resort & Spa and a giant campground. That big campground was the staging area for the Wild Goose Festival, part Woodstock, part Burning Man, part South by Southwest (SXSW) and 100 percent progressive Christian.

It's a place where you see banners like "Who Would Jesus Torture?" and "Recovering From Religion." Another intertwined hearts and the words "Jesus and Darwin" in a line drawing of a fish used to symbolize Christianity.

Religion has always wrestled with sex in this nation. Sex is something that tempts you, gets you in to trouble. So if there were anywhere in the country where I would hear a minister talk about the joy of sex, this was it.

And Bolz-Weber did not fail me. She is the founder of the House for All Sinners and Saints in Denver, Colorado, which caters to those on the margins, and a *New York Times* best-selling author. She gave a deliciously profanity-laced talk about her latest book, *Shameless: A Sexual Reformation*. Martin Luther must be spinning in his grave! I'd thought when I first saw that title. Her take on sex and Christianity was music to my ears. Christianity, in my experience, has always had a big problem with sex. You need it to propagate the species, but it's just a little too much fun to be good on its own. At the festival, Bolz-Weber did a major league deep dive into talking about the joys of shame-free sex, cutting the bonds that religion has tied around the joy of sex.

Some parts of her talk were painful. That was when she described the end of her marriage and the start of a relationship with her new boyfriend. One reason she ended her marriage was because of sex. Or rather, lack of it. Or not enough of it. I actually can't remember exactly what she said because, instead of her voice, I heard my soon-to-be ex-husband's voice telling me roughly the same thing about our sex life and that he had no more time to put into it. Or our marriage. That hurt. Because I had put so much time and effort into that marriage. And into him. And that included trying to revive our sex life. Because I love sex.

In high school, my wiry, blond, Norwegian Lutheran boyfriend and I had torrid make-out sessions in his red Barracuda on county trunk roads up on the Ridge, hills that ringed Sparta, the small Wisconsin farm town where I grew up. We'd drive up Highway 71 towards Norwalk or Highway 27 toward Cashton, two little villages, passing barns, farmyards and fields of corn and hay. Heading uphill to the Ridge, the highways pass through stands of scrub pine and oak trees and then to the top, where the roads travel along the spine of the Ridge. It's a stupendous view of seemingly endless sky, rolling farmland dipping down into forested valleys, with the occasional Amish horse-drawn buggy clip-clopping along.

Of course, we weren't up there for the view.

At the drive-in movies, we were horizontal in the front seat and making out before the previews had ended, oblivious to whatever the couple double dating with us was doing in the back seat. His older sister let us use her apartment! Major score for high schoolers! I'd bought some book packed with ideas like squirting Reddi wip on each other for a little additional fun during oral sex. It made us both giggle. We were two small-town kids too afraid to buy condoms at the local drugstore, which sat on the main intersection of downtown Sparta next to the town's only stop-and-go light. My family's next-door neighbor ran that drugstore. So, blow jobs and oral sex were as far as we would go.

There were more boyfriends after that, in college, in the small town where I had my first full-time job as a reporter, in Aspen where one of my best friends from college and I spent a season ski bumming and, finally, grad school in New York.

There, I dated a couple of Columbia College English majors looking for their Molly Bloom, heroine of James Joyce's Ulysses. It seemed to have been a core part of their curriculum. One of them thought he'd found her in me. Except that once I discovered what I thought was the high calorie count of seminal fluid (it's apparently fairly low in calories, I've since learned), I started to spit it out. A very un-Molly move, he told me, laughing. I was also very un-Molly in that I only took one lover at a time.

Finally, at a party, I met the guy I would eventually marry. He was slim and tautly muscled, olive skinned, with curly black hair and gorgeous hazel eyes. He was funny, sarcastic and totally unlike any of my other boyfriends. We met once and then, not again, for months. But we became part of an informal group of twenty- and thirty-somethings who loved concerts in Central Park, hiking, skiing, cooking, eating and drinking. I called us the Outdoors Sports and Photo Op Club because we'd have parties to look at photos after our weekend adventures in those pre-digital photo days.

And, boy, was he an emotionally armored guy. But when we first kissed in his apartment, I stuck my tongue in his mouth. I got his attention. He already had mine. I loved him, blindly. We moved in together and bought our first apartment. I bored my coworkers as I rhapsodized about him and my adventures with New York real estate.

It was fun and wonderful. There were lots of evenings of stopping for a bottle of wine on the way home from work and cooking dinner together before crashing into bed. I loved sitting at my desk at work and smelling his musky maleness on my skin. It came from a quick morning tumble that dictated a too quick shower that couldn't quite wash away his scent.

Years went by.

Marriage, kids, mortgages. I had always felt that sex in the morning would guarantee a solid marriage. I just hadn't factored in the exhaustion of work, freelance writing, cooking, lick-and-a-promise cleaning and getting kids to skating lessons, swimming lessons, horseback riding lessons, Hebrew school and on and on and on.

The result? Those encounters didn't happen nearly often enough. And it wasn't just kids, too many hours at work, too little time at home and not enough money. It was all the baggage we all carry. Things can be falling apart and you can still have good sex short term. But sooner or later, what's happening in other parts of your relationship catches up with sex and overtakes it. And that is what had happened between me and the driven, sexy, funny, depressed, angry and, in his deepest depths, terrified man I'd married.

Those memories kept playing in the back of my head as I listened to Bolz-Weber. A lot of what she said went straight to my wounded heart and made it feel better. She talked about an ex-boyfriend who would routinely insult her — and then worry that the squirrels in a park wouldn't have enough to eat. I knew that bewildering combination of cruelty and kindness all too well. This talk riveted me.

Bolz-Weber was fearless enough to talk — and write — about her abortion. In one of her books (I read *Shameless* and *Accidental Saints: Finding God in All the Wrong People* over the weekend and on my flight home, and *Pastrix: The Cranky, Beautiful Faith of a Sinner and a Saint* as soon as I got home) she wrote about how she had always loved babies, starting with the infant her family had fostered when Bolz-Weber was just twelve. He was her baby. She doted on him and checked to make sure he was still breathing. As a twelve-year-old, I had doted on my own baby brother in exactly the same way. He was a real live baby doll for my sister and me and our friends. But Bolz-Weber's little baby was only on loan to her family. *Don't get too attached*, her mother had warned her. But she had.

Years later, when Bolz-Weber discovered she was pregnant, she was broke and newly sober. She knew she couldn't take care of this baby. And she knew she could not give it to someone else to raise. She had an abortion.

She was a preacher who won me over with her honesty and vulnerability. And as the battle-scarred veteran of three different religions, I was a hard sell.

Even Visa knew I was a religious skeptic. It declined the charge when I tried to book my trip to the festival. Kate Rice go to a Christian event? Must be fraud! As I used my American Express card to book my accommodations — a tent — my younger daughter made fun of me.

"Mama's glamping for Jesus," she wickedly texted her big sister.

What the hell was I, a totally secular, sneak-out-of-Mass-at-Communion-lapsed-Catholic, social-justice-only-converted-Jew and liberal from the Democratic bastion of New York City doing at a Christian festival in the South?

Ostensibly, I was trying to sell a book I'd written about refugee resettlement. When refugees swept across Europe in 2015, I, like so many others in this often big-hearted nation, had dived in to do what I could to help at least a few refugees. In the process, I had become a charter member of my New York City synagogue's new refugee resettlement committee, the B'nai Jeshurun refugee committee. On top of that, I got involved with Rutgers Presbyterian Church, just a block and a half from my apartment. Rutgers managed to resettle not one but two refugee families from Syria. Rutgers' volunteers started getting calls from other congregations asking how they had done it; I kept telling them they needed to write it down and share it.

They were too busy. Then I reminded myself, "I'm a reporter! I can write it!" So I went to work.

Because I wanted the book to resonate with people outside my Upper West Side liberal enclave, I searched for and found congregations in the Bible Belt and other red states — solid Trump territory — who were working with refugees. Some were even lobbying their Republican representatives in Washington, DC, urging them to push President Trump to let more refugees into the country.

It was the perfect story for me, a big-city Democrat with roots in a rural, purple-to-red corner of Wisconsin. It was a counter-intuitive story about an issue that was polarizing in the headlines but unifying on the ground among everyday Americans from across the political spectrum. In post-2016 America, I wanted secular people like me — suspicious of the overtly religious because of the hypocrisy of many members of the religious right — to know that they had allies in an unlikely place: Christian churches.

In most of the places I did interviews, Arkansas, California, Idaho, Iowa, Kentucky, North Carolina, Texas, Utah and elsewhere, I found people of faith — some of them from very conservative congregations, working with the secular and the liberal. A friend of a friend had suggested that the annual Wild Goose Festival, which began in 2011 and now attracted thousands of progressive Christians, was the perfect place for the author of a book like mine.

I'd never heard of the Wild Goose, so I researched it. It calls itself a spirit, justice, music and arts festival with roots in progressive Christianity. That means it's not just about belief. It's about social justice and love, welcoming everyone. And I mean everyone. Whatever your age, race, gender, sexual orientation, religious tradition, whatever your abilities or disabilities, you are welcome. If you have strong faith or no faith, you are welcome. If you have a million questions about faith, you're welcome.

The Wild Goose took its inspiration from the Greenbelt Festival, an English festival that was about music, social justice and spirituality. Its organizers also looked to Burning Man, Lightning in a Bottle and SXSW festivals for ideas.

Why call it the Wild Goose Festival? Because a wild goose is strong, beautiful and utterly unpredictable. The Wild Goose Festival's organizers believe that, like the wild goose, the Holy Spirit can surprise you and take you down unexpected — and often totally disruptive —paths.

I liked that. I was looking for alternative paths. Disruption had become a way of life for me — and not by choice. Using the Wild Goose Festival as a venue for selling my book really was just an excuse.

I felt a little like a refugee myself. Now, to be clear, I am making no comparison between the desperate plight of the seventy million displaced people on the earth today and my situation. I wasn't escaping war, famine or people trying to kill me. I was trying to escape the emotional devastation of a long-disintegrating marriage in its death throes. A meteor had crashed into my world, laying waste to the landscape of my life. Instead of a lush, Technicolor world of happiness, it was a place of smoldering ashes, burned-out trees and pain.

For far too long that marriage had been among those all-too-common ones that looked fine from the outside. I focused on the good parts only. That was the only story I told to myself, my daughters and my friends and family. But that story held only if you didn't look too close. And some people saw the truth.

"How can you live with him?" one of his work colleagues once asked when she bumped into me on the street. After a friend saw him explode in anger, she asked me out for drinks. "Are you safe?" she asked. "You can come stay with us."

"Does he always talk to you like that?" someone else asked. "That is *not* okay."

His cutting words could break up a dinner party, provoke a neighbor to storm out of our co-op building's board meeting and eviscerate servers with his criticisms of the restaurant's kitchen, menu and service.

But I pretended he left that dark, angry man at the door when he came home. That he was kind and loving with us. Which he could be! But he was wildly unpredictable. I walked on eggshells. I never knew what might provoke his lacerating tongue and explosive temper. Sometimes things would literally explode. Like the family camping trip that followed what had been a frustrating week for him at work. It was a rainy night, and he couldn't get the soggy wood to burn. I looked at the cheery campfires crackling away at sites around us and said, "Maybe try putting a little cookstove fuel on the fire?"

He looked straight at me and poured an entire container of cook stove fuel on the smoldering logs.

Flames shot up into the treetops. Conversations in the surrounding campsites halted. I jumped back, gasping in shock. Everyone stared at us.

"You told me to do it," he said.

He never hit me. But I always felt a sense of a barely restrained, underlying violence.

I clung to the memory of the wonderful relationship he and I had once had, in part because I so wanted to believe he was the Prince Charming he seemed to have been in those first years.

And he had been Prince Charming. Early in our relationship, he went on a cross-country trip to climb the Grand Tetons in Wyoming. Every day, he sent me a postcard. I still have them.

At work, he'd fax me page after page filled with nothing but "I love you." I kept one.

I was a reporter, and the ski industry was one of my beats. I went on a work trip to Vail with a slew of ski professionals for the opening of some newly developed back bowls. I came back from a night of partying with ski bums to find he'd sent a bouquet of roses; they awaited me in my room.

He was a Jew who didn't do Christmas; he told me when we first met. I was so relieved! Because that first year, I had no idea of what to get him. Then, of course, he gave me a smashing gift. I now can't remember what it was. I can only remember how it made me feel. Treasured. Whatever it was, it was something I wanted but had told no one about. I felt seen in a way I had never been seen before. By anyone. Ever. It seemed to fill a hole in me that I hadn't known was there.

On the sidewalk in front of the apartment we had bought on New York's Upper West Side, the city poured concrete around a tree out front. He took a stick, wrote our initials into the still-soft concrete, and drew the outline of a heart around it.

I once came home to a massive valentine, a giant heart drawn on four pieces of printing paper, taped together. I still have that. On it, he'd written K + G. 4 Ever.

Actually. Not 4 Ever. Obviously. Still, those deposits in our relationship bank paid dividends for a long, long time, offsetting the way he'd put me down or put down friends and neighbors with his cutting tongue. He could be funny as hell. Once I blew out my back, badly. One night I carefully lowered myself onto our bed, carefully swinging my feet up on the bed and then slowly lying down, heaving a huge sigh of relief at the end of the laborious process.

He was already in bed, reading. He put down his book, turned to me and said, "Wanna fool around?"

I howled with laughter, wincing at the same time because it

hurt my back. "Don't make me laugh!" I begged. But I kept laughing.

Those moments of sweetness and humor offset his pushing me, a writer, to become a financial planner or a real estate agent, so I'd make more money.

And we needed more money. The Internet with its user-generated content had blown up my once-lucrative freelance business. That free user content cut demand for the freelancing that had helped us fund our apartment purchases on the Upper West Side. My income dropped just as our bills shot up. He started making more money—and expected me to keep up. "We never talked about that," I protested. "It was implicit," he countered. We had one and then two kids in private school, something I had resisted. We had one of the top elementary schools in the city just a few blocks away from us. I wanted to save private school for middle and upper school. But he pushed so relentlessly that I finally gave in. Those schools charged tuitions that ultimately came to $45K a year. Per kid.

So, of course, I also felt too broke to leave.

He promised me that we could make it work. I made myself believe him when he said he loved me and was committed to me. But he didn't act like it. He was angry because, ultimately, I had rejected what he considered a core part of himself: his depression and anger. And he saw I was no longer willing to let him take it out on our family and use us as human antidepressants.

I could see his crushing pain. And I was sorry that he suffered so. I so wanted him to be free of his depression. Because then he could be what I thought was the true him: funny, smart, sweet, sentimental. But I couldn't cut his depression and pain out of him. And he couldn't. Or wouldn't. "It's who I am," he said. He withdrew, slowly but inexorably, from the marriage and from me.

"He never really seemed to trust in the process," one of the five therapists we saw over those years told me later. It ended in a firestorm that burned away all of my illusions about my world and about myself.

When we stood outside of that last therapist's office after he and the therapist had told me my husband was done with the marriage, I felt homeless.

"Why are you looking at me like that?" he asked.

I couldn't say anything. All I could think was I had no money and no home. And who was this stranger standing in front of me?

It turned out that I would be the one to stay in the Upper West Side apartment that he and I had built together, buying and combining three apartments into one over the years. But I was really just the caretaker. One of the few things that everyone agreed on — him, me and the judge handling our case — was that we would not sell the apartment until our youngest, soon to be a high school senior, left for college.

I gutted the apartment of his stuff — filling a storeroom not once but twice with his belongings, cataloging and photographing the contents of each box as if it were a museum collection (the Virgo in me doesn't come out often, but when she does, it's Katie bar the door!) He'd haul it away and I'd fill it again. The apartment felt much cleaner and more open, but for me, it felt haunted. The ghosts of the hopeful young lovers he and I once had been flitted about. Shattered dreams crunched like shards of broken lightbulbs under my feet.

Refugees become refugees because they don't have a home anymore. It's been destroyed, or it is too dangerous to stay in. They flee death and destruction and refugees can't pick their escape route. They just pick whatever route looks open. What had once been my home now felt to me like a smoking ruin. Like a refugee, I started taking any road that opened up before me. If there wasn't gate across it, I took it.

So I registered for the Wild Goose Festival.

I studied the event website and found a healthy emphasis on beer. There were multiple Beer and Hymns sessions and even a Beer Theology session. *Amen to that*, I thought! That eased my fears that there would be a lot of sessions with earnest people holding hands, praying and singing. If there were, it looked as though I'd be able to keep at least one hand free for a beer.

Given I didn't know anyone else who was attending, I decided to find community by signing on as a volunteer. I landed on the ticketing team, the people who admit the approximately four thousand attendees.

There are a couple of different Jesuses out there. One Jesus would have us believe the Bible literally, fight abortion, defend the family — which has to be straight — and would damn to hell everyone who doesn't toe the party line. There's another Jesus. This Jesus is an open-hearted guy. He's about love, loving everyone and including everyone in that love, and reaching out to the other.

That openness permeated the Wild Goose Festival. Everywhere I went, I fell into straightforward conversations. Many people there were recovering from religious trauma. Recovering from a religion that taught kids to feel ashamed of their sexual longings, recovering from sexual abuse in the church, recovering from a religion worshipping a vengeful and angry God.

I felt as though I fit right in; I was recovering from a marriage in which I felt constantly undermined and demeaned. Religion had been one of the weapons my husband had used against me. He'd berate me for my imperfect embrace of Judaism; it was part of a list of shortcomings he relentlessly catalogued for me. It was such a relief to be surrounded by people unafraid to show their wounds — and their commitment to healing.

My volunteering meant I kept talking to new people. One night I helped wash dishes after a dinner for hundreds. Our outdoor kitchen overlooked the muddy waters of the French Broad River as it rushed by the campground on its way to the Tennessee River. My washing-and-drying partner had come of age in the 90s in a part of Georgia where being Christian means you are a conservative Christian. As an adult, she rejected that religion. She gave up on God, because; she told me, the God she was raised on wasn't a God of love. Then she discovered progressive Christianity and its loving God.

Another night I met Nate Novero, a docu-series producer and former Southern Baptist minister. He described the trauma caused by the purity culture, the extreme chastity movement that scaled up in the 1990s. It spawned massive events in stadiums across the country that sold abstinence to young people. Christian rock stars performed, providing a soundtrack to not have sex to. And thousands of people in their teens and twenties learned to be ashamed of their bodies and their God-given sex drives. Then, once they were in a straight marriage, sex would magically be okay. It didn't work like that at all for Nate and his ex-wife. So now, he was tackling healing that trauma, for himself and others, with his camera and with a podcast called The Touch about religion and sex.

"You're doing a podcast about religion and sex?" I repeated his words, not really believing my ears.

"Yes," he'd replied, laughing.

The Wild Goose Festival was a sanctuary. Volunteers had written "Love Heals" on the hard-boiled eggs I'd grab for a quick breakfast after my run.

At the entry gate one day, two women arrived. They had driven straight through from Colorado. As a volunteer scanned their tickets, the women wept, overjoyed to be with kindred souls.

Wow, I thought, getting a glimpse of what it must be like to be a person of faith when the religious right has hijacked your God.

A lot of Subarus pulled in, but there were a lot of trucks, too. After a giant red Ram truck arrived and we had waved its occupants through, one of my team members, Jes Miller, (my dance partner after Bolz-Weber's talk) turned to me and said, "Now that was not what I expected to see here."

Me neither.

As the weekend wore on, the ticketing team had less to do and more time to talk. One, a tall, white man with a soft Southern accent, talked about his keen awareness of the advantages of being straight, white and male.

I had dinner with my two of my "glamping" neighbors, Trevor and John. Both were youth ministers and they talked about the workshops they'd taken that day. One workshop had focused on post-colonialism and the role churches played. That led to talking about the politicization of churches, which led to talking about abortion and racism.

Hmm, I thought, *so much of what we hear about religion today is about believing. Believe the right thing and you'll get into heaven. Not here. Here it was about doing, trying to make heaven right here on earth.*

I didn't sell any books at the Goose. I didn't find Jesus. I still felt fragile as hell.

But, I had found one helluva story.

The multidenominational, polyglot and long-overlooked progressive Christian movement.

And by God, I intended to write the book about it.

2

HIJACKING JESUS

I grew up with an Irish Catholic dad and an Episcopalian WASP mother.

We never talked about Jesus. Most of my Catholic friends didn't either.

If there were any deity us Catholic kids worshipped, it was the Blessed Virgin Mary (BVM). I know, she's a saint, she's not God (although some unkind Protestants used to say Catholics treated her like God), but the nuns taught us to pray to her, probably because a mother figure is more approachable than God. I still pray to the BVM on bumpy airline flights.

My friends who were Lutheran, Methodist, Congregationalist, or other mainstream Protestant denominations didn't talk about Jesus either, or the BVM, of course. My Protestant friends went to Sunday school and worked at church dinners at their mothers' sides. Not that we didn't believe in God, or that religion wasn't important to us. It was woven into our lives.

My family said grace before each meal. But true to Rice irreverence, we'd end the Sign of the Cross by saying "In the name of the Father, the Son and the Holy Spirit, amen." At "amen," we'd all clap our hands together once. We still do — including my daughters, who I raised as Jews.

When I'd walk past my parents' room on my way to bed at night, Dad would be on his knees, saying his prayers. To be honest, I do the same at night. I'm not on my knees, I'm in bed, staring into the darkness and praying for my kids, my family and the world—harder than ever, frankly. Maybe not to God explicitly, but to some force bigger than I am that I can feel out there.

My sister, my brothers, and I started our religious careers with my mother, who went to St. John's Episcopal Church. She was very active in her church. It was small, had an aging congregation, and all of its members doted on us kids. My mother baked rolls for church dinners and created lovely centerpieces. We helped set the tables. In the 1960 presidential campaign, my toddler brother met Jacqueline Kennedy when she made a campaign stop in my hometown and visited St. John's.

Once we hit Holy Communion age, we transitioned over to St. Patrick's Catholic Church. We went to church every Sunday morning or Saturday night, first with Dad, and then, as we got older, on our own, slipping out (at least in my case) when we could after Holy Communion. We suffered through catechism class on Saturday mornings in elementary school and Confraternity of Christian Doctrine (CCD) classes every Wednesday night in high school. By that point, I was arguing with teachers and the priest, Father Thomas Garthwaite, over the legality of abortion. I was pro choice, and of course, he was anti-abortion.

"Does your father know you think like this?" Father Garthwaite demanded.

He certainly did. In fact, he agreed with me.

My dad was an Irish Catholic Democrat.

He went to Mass every day at St. Patrick's. Just as his father had.

One of my brothers says it's because Dad was county judge.

Dad loved applying theory to reality. He thought—before law school became prohibitively expensive—that anyone who could should go to law school for the way it trained your brain.

But it wasn't just the legal theory that made him love his job. He loved all the people and their stories, the drama and the comedy. Every day, he made decisions that changed lives: granting divorces, putting people in jail, taking children away from their parents. He got to know a lot of people very well. And, he cared. A telling example of this was a kid who was in and out of Dad's court throughout his adolescence. When the kid grew up and got married, he had my dad officiate at his wedding. Dad had been one of the few reliable adults in his life.

Of course, not everybody who went through Dad's court appreciated him. Once Dad was looking out the courtroom window, listening to testimony from a man getting divorced. A guy walked out of the county jail. He'd just been released. He looked up at the courtroom window and he gave Dad the finger. Dad cracked up, to the bewilderment of the poor guy still testifying. Dad was sorry about that. He had a little note on his desk that read. "Be polite. Always." But sometimes he had to laugh.

Another time he sentenced a guy, and the guy panicked, running to that same second-floor window, trying to jump out. Dad, a runner, leaped down from the bench, his black robe flying out behind him, and grabbed him before the bailiffs got there.

"He looked just like Batman swooping down," said the clerk of courts, admiringly.

It wasn't all small-town stuff. Sometimes, he was sent to Milwaukee County to help clean up its backlogs. He was an efficient judge. And back in the 70s, when the mob still ruled, and the courts fought it, Milwaukee County would assign him to some of those cases. He didn't tell us much about those, but I remember one story about a hit, and then how the killers urinated on the victim.

Sometimes my mother would join him in Milwaukee at the end of those weeks, leaving the five of us with a babysitter. That meant they could have an adults-only weekend. One night they walked into an Italian restaurant. Dad took one look at the maître d' and did an about-face, steering my mother right back out the door.

That maître d' was freshly out of the prison Dad had sent him to.

Sometimes, the world came to Dad's courtroom. Which is exactly what happened in 1980. That spring and summer, 125,000 Cubans fled their country in a flotilla of boats and rafts. As would happen in the Mediterranean thirty-five years later, men, women and children packed onto overcrowded vessels, many of them of questionable seaworthiness; twenty-seven died on the 125-mile trip from Cuba to Florida.[1]

The exodus riveted the nation. Fear wrestled with compassion. In 1980, it wasn't extremists who frightened Americans; it was, instead, the fact that Fidel Castro had emptied his prisons and mental health institutions, releasing inmates to join the flow of refugees.

An overwhelming number of boat people flooded Florida's shores, and the federal government sent thousands for additional processing to federal installations across the United States.

One of those installations was Fort McCoy, a military base on sixty thousand acres of rolling hills covered with pine woods, streams and ponds in Monroe County, where my hometown was the county seat.

That's when Dad took on what was then the US Immigration and Naturalization Service (INS). (In 2003, the INS became part of the US Citizenship and Naturalization Services, and now includes Immigration and Customs Enforcement and Customs and Border Protection).

The national news media descended on Monroe County. As soon as he heard that Fort McCoy would be a processing center, Dad contacted U.S. Attorney Frank Teurkheimer in Madison for all the information he could get on federal immigration law. He became a constant and outspoken critic of the refugee center and fought the feds whenever he felt they were overstepping their jurisdiction. When Fort McCoy military police started to stop and search cars on Highway 21, which cuts through McCoy, Dad refused to allow the MPs to search his 1963 Studebaker truck.

"It's a state highway. Not your jurisdiction!" he barked at the young MP who'd flagged us down. He shifted gears on the truck and it chugged off. I sat beside him, gasping with horror and delight as he, a staunch Democrat, asserted states' rights from his rattletrap truck.

Almost immediately, Dad began hearing troubling stories coming out of Fort McCoy — reports that unaccompanied minors were being physically and sexually assaulted. As a county judge, he had no jurisdiction on a military base — but off the base, he did. He quietly spread the word.

Two courageous Good Samaritans, a civilian worker and an Army major, smuggled a couple of kids out. They dropped one off on our front porch. Bingo. They became children in need of protection and services from the state of Wisconsin. Dad placed one in a local shelter and sent the other to the child's relatives in Florida. An outraged INS threatened to arrest the kids as illegal aliens. But Dad stood firm. The INS also took those Good Samaritans to court, but ultimately dropped charges. Dad always said the civilian worker and the Army major were the real heroes. Dad, along with Judge Ness Flores of Waukesha

County, presided over hearings for forty-nine juveniles. His only regret: that he could not help more.

He was integral to an overhaul of the Wisconsin state court system in the 1970s. He was part of a movement that brought new efficiencies to an aging state court system. He made his username his license plate number: JDG228, which was quite handy for me when I was a teenager doing a little underage drinking. A friend and I were using my dad's car and were on a rural road drinking beer when the cops saw us. They knew whatever we were doing was illegal or possibly immoral. But they didn't bust us. They just flashed a warning light and made an announcement over the loudspeaker. "Put on your parking lights."

Dad worked well with the cops. They'd complain about each other — he was the guy who would apply the law to the messy real-life situations that the cops dealt with. But they respected each other as well. Dad knew cops were people, most were good, some were bad. One of his great partners was Ray Harris, who was Monroe County sheriff for years. Ray rode a Harley-Davidson, wore cowboy boots and big belt buckles, and talked like the good ol' boy from the South that he was. Dad had been a ski jumper in his youth, wore Brooks Brothers suits, ran and was a cross-country skier. They could hardly have looked more different, but they both had big hearts and worked hand in hand.

When Dad died, the entire Monroe County sheriff's department lined the steps of St. Pat's for his funeral. They snapped to attention and saluted as my mother, my siblings and I walked between them up the steps and into the church. All the sitting justices on the Wisconsin Supreme Court were inside waiting for us. It was a good place for the people he had worked so closely with to say goodbye to him. The reason Dad went to church every day was because there was no way in hell that he could do a job that big all by himself.

My dad was an intensely religious man who turned to church and God for wisdom and solace. But he was equally intense about keeping his faith private. The only way you knew about his faith was if you were in church or a prayer retreat with him. If you weren't there, you had no idea of the strength of his faith. He was a sociable, funny guy who was friends with everyone — Democrats and Republicans, farmers and store owners, kids and adults. He was tolerant. He was the kind of guy who would leave a party given by the social workers running a halfway house early so they could smoke pot.

I feel he epitomized mainstream religion — devout, but private, a true believer who respected the belief of others. Someone who devoted his life to making the world a better place for everyone, especially those outside Jesus' proverbial tent. My dad was a man who used his belief in God to power his work on this earth, to make it better for all, as opposed to letting his belief define his world and who could be in it.

Unlike far right Christians, who focus on belief and how it gets you into heaven and woe unto you if you do not toe the company line, progressive Protestant churches and social-justice minded Catholics like my dad believe in individualism and bearing social witness.[2] They don't try to make their religion their core identity. They, and the churches where they worship, encourage freedom of thought.

This is in stark contrast to the way many evangelicals live in their silos, reading their own books and associating only with those who think the way they do. Certainly, they contribute to their communities — running food kitchens, helping Habitat for Humanity and similar excellent efforts. But their mindset is very different.

Bradley Onishi, associate professor of religion at Skidmore College and co-host of a podcast I highly recommend, *Straight White American Jesus*, laid out the difference between conservative evangelicals and progressive Christians. Progressive Christians are open to the world and embrace society at large. That openness gave the political right an advantage when it came to claiming Jesus.

"There's a paradox for mainline Protestants and what I would call socially minded Catholics," he told me in an interview right after Joe Biden won the 2020 election and it was clear that the nation was going to face continuing challenges from the religious right.

In the late nineteenth century and early twentieth century, mainline Protestants saw themselves as accommodating culture. They adapted to the changing world. So mainline Protestants mostly accepted the theory of evolution — they could accept evolution and still believe in God.

Accommodating culture meant that, during the 20th century, they supported the women's suffrage movement, pushed for child labor laws and were part of some of the first pushes for sexual health education, Onishi said.

Ultimately, they were instrumental in the civil rights movement. In short, mainline Protestants and a lot of Catholics (like my dad and the rest of my family) adopted what's called the social gospel.

"Instead of going out into the world to make converts, to proselytize, to convert their neighbors or people far afield or in other countries, mainline Protestants saw their faith as creating a more equal, just and inclusive society," Onishi said.

It's not about getting into heaven. It's about making life better right here on earth right now.

That, Onishi said, understands the message of Jesus to be about helping the outcast, the marginalized, the poor, those in need, the stranger. It's about seeing justice done and fighting for equality. What was then called the social gospel movement dates to the late 1800s. Among its adherents accomplishments:

settlement houses to help immigrants and the poor, the eight-hour workday and abolishing child labor.

In the early twentieth century, Walter Rauschenbusch, a Baptist who was the pastor of an immigrant church in New York's Hell's Kitchen, took this movement further. In his 1907 book *Christianity and the Social Crisis,* he wrote that religion's purpose was to create the best life possible for all citizens, which became the foundation for religion addressing problems like economic inequality, racism and militarism.[3]

That tradition continued through the decades. It grew into a religious progressivism centered on openness and inclusiveness. But this also weakened the Christian progressive brand. Here's why.

Christian progressives work (or worked) on many social justice fronts. If you were part of this group, you weren't flying the flag of your faith. You were flying the flag of the cause you advocated for.

You're going to stand side by side with LGBTQ plus activists, advocates for refugees and immigrants, and protestors calling for equal rights for people of color and for reproductive freedom.

Your religious identity is just one of many things that define you. And the world doesn't see you as progressive Protestants or social justice-minded Catholics; it may just see you as activists fighting for economic, racial or social justice.

"One of the paradoxes of the story is that they were so successful they kind of became invisible," Onishi said.

He calls this victorious invisibility. That means that the child of a mainline Protestant preacher in 1965 can grow into an adult who says to herself, "Y'know, I can fight these battles without having to brand myself as a Methodist or a Baptist."

Social justice movements and progressive Christians tend to have common beliefs about justice, inclusivity, equality and giving a helping hand. Social justice movements include many people of faith.

Here is one historic example. Religious leaders from a variety of denominations were integral to the passing of landmark civil rights legislation in the early 1960s. Hubert Humphrey, the Democratic senator from Minnesota who helped shepherd that landmark legislation through the Senate, gave churches a huge amount of credit for their work These were people of faith who did not push their beliefs on others or imprint their religious brand on those movements. These progressive Christians saw they didn't need to fight for these great causes under any religious labels like being Methodist or Baptist.

Onishi took the perspective of someone like this in order to explain it to me.

"Maybe over time I retain the morals and the principles that I learned from my church, but maybe I've stopped going. Maybe it's not really part of my life. Maybe I no longer identify that way," he said.

As these progressives drifted away from the church, mainline Protestantism declined. Progressives were less tied to a religious identity — and churches lost money.

"So what we see over the course of the last part of the twentieth century is a precipitous decline of mainline Protestantism in terms of influence, visibility and money," said Onishi. "Many of the seminaries are closing. Many of the colleges have lost their economic viability."

Churches closed or merged.

As this was happening, evangelicalism launched its branding wars. The religious right did not hesitate to use God's name and its churches to try to make abortion illegal, fight gun safety legislation and deny climate change.

When you view mainstreamers through that kind of prism,

it's easier to understand how mainstream denominations' openness to those of other beliefs put them at a disadvantage when compared with the religious right's successful effort to brand Christianity in its own image.

I came from that tradition of openness and inclusivity.

Although we were a church-going family, we didn't talk much about God.

The people we mainstream religious kids most commonly heard talk about God or Jesus were the guys (and back in the 60s and 70s it was always a guy) standing at the pulpit on Sunday morning and the nuns and Sunday school teachers.

In high school CCD classes, one of my classmates talked about Roman Catholicism as being the "best religion." That made me squirm. Religion, I believed, was man-made. I believed that there were many routes to God, and churches provided us with many paths. No one church provided the best way, in my view, and I was pretty sure anyone could talk to God without coaching from any church.

We also never talked about Jesus in my house. The only time you'd hear his name was if someone hit a thumb with a hammer or if we were talking about some Republican policy that made us mad.

However, some of my friends did talk about Jesus. They were usually Assembly of God, Southern Baptist or Seventh Day Adventist. Jesus was their buddy. They talked to him; they even got advice from him.

I remember sitting in violin class in seventh or eighth grade and listening to a classmate whose dad was a Baptist preacher and whose mom played piano for the church choir. Every once in a while, she'd talk earnestly about some of her family's religious views. And that made me a little uncomfortable. She wasn't proselytizing. But she just talked about God a little more than anyone in my family did. It didn't help that, unlike me, she had always practiced her violin and always had her homework done. She had a great sense of humor, we were friends, and we went to a lot of the same slumber parties, but there was always just a tiny little space, just a slight hesitation between those who talked directly to Jesus and us mainstreamers.

The way we kids in school worked was something like the way the nation worked. The fact that we didn't talk about God outside of church or our own prayers made it easy for conservative Christians to hijack Jesus and claim him as Republican.

While progressive denominations were participating in the world, fighting for the rights of all, the religious right was focusing on declaring its God was the true God and that God opposed abortion (and a lot of other reproductive rights), homosexuality (yes, God loved you if you were gay, but would still send you to hell if you didn't adopt a straight lifestyle), and that those who did not embrace those beliefs 100 percent were damned. Democrats were guaranteed to go to hell and would probably do their best to take as many true Christians as possible with them. Today, if you hear the word religious, most people picture evangelicals or fundamentalists.

When Onishi asks students in his classes to name a famous Christian in the United States, they always name evangelicals. They used to name Tim Tebow, a football star who was the son of Baptist missionaries and spoke publicly about his faith, and President George W. Bush. Now, they name Justin Bieber and Chris Pratt.

But they don't name Stacey Abrams, daughter of two Methodist ministers whose beliefs have formed her life and work. They don't name Elizabeth Warren, who was raised Methodist, taught Sunday school, and who often says that her favorite biblical passage is Matthew 25:40, in which Jesus urges his followers to care for the marginalized, saying, "When you did it to the least of these brothers, you did it to me." They don't name Joe Biden, who goes to church every Sunday. His religion, I believe, is clearly central to who he is, as it was for my dad. For both men, religion drove their principles, morals and their lives.

Perhaps that's because Warren, Abrams, Biden, my dad and so many other progressive people of faith, are about inclusiveness and love. Not hate.

In contrast, evangelicals have mostly created a world of their own, one that requires its members to literally go by the book or get kicked out into a world that is full of (shudder) Democrats and other infidels who will face eternity in hell and will probably drag you down with them.

Ultimately, evangelicalism turned into one of the biggest, tightest silos ever.

Silos dot the landscape of Monroe County. Silos are where farmers store corn and other grains that they'll ultimately use to feed livestock. Farmers seal them to keep the grain fresh. These stored grains ferment and emit silo gases that help keep those grains fresh. However, those gases often include a lot of carbon monoxide, and, during a critical period when the silage is first stored, those gases can be lethal. Carbon monoxide replaces the oxygen in our blood and, at sufficient quantities, suffocates us.

The religious right's doctrinaire focus on a rigorously defined belief pushes away independent thought. The result: fear. Fear of hell, of temptation, of nonbelievers who might tempt you or corrupt your children. It's a movement that tamps down critical thinking, insists on unquestioning belief, grooming its members for authoritarian rulers and autocrats.

That siloing started after the 1925 Scopes trial, dramatized in the 1960s movie *Inherit the Wind* as a parable about McCarthyism. Joe McCarthy was a senator from (sigh) my home state of Wisconsin who made political hay demonizing government officials, academics, labor leaders and members of the entertainment industry, branding them as Communist sympathizers. It was a movement that flourished in the 1950s and destroyed careers and lives.

The movie version of *Inherit the Wind* was adapted from the 1955 play with the same name. Nedrick Young, the film's co-writer, wrote the screenplay under a pseudonym, because he'd been blacklisted as a Communist.

In real life, a young teacher named John Scopes agreed to teach evolution to test a state law that banned the teaching of evolution. It was a contradictory law, because the state-approved science textbook included the teaching of evolution.

Bang. Science and the Bible went *mano-a-mano* in a wrestling match at a court in Dayton, Tennessee. It played out in real time for the American public to hear over live radio broadcasts straight from the courtroom.

William Jennings Bryan, three-time Democratic presidential candidate and nationally famous orator from Nebraska, was the prosecutor. History has mixed views of Bryan, but there is no denying his influence during America's progressive era, which ran roughly from the 1890s to the 1920s, an era of social activism and reform that was a response to problems caused by industrialization, urbanization and immigration.

Bryan was Secretary of State in President Woodrow Wilson's administration but he resigned in 1915 and focused more on religious and anti-evolution efforts.

Clarence Darrow defended John Scopes. Darrow's father had been an abolitionist and a religious freethinker whom his neighbors had called "the village infidel." His mother supported women's right to vote and women's rights. Darrow, known as the sophisticated country lawyer, helped start the Progressive Party in Illinois and ran unsuccessfully for Congress as a Democrat. He was an anti-imperialist who opposed the US annexation of the Philippines and was a labor lawyer who represented woodworkers in Wisconsin and striking coal miners in Pennsylvania. He was a leading member of the American Civil Liberties Union. He had his brushes with infamy. He was once accused of trying to bribe a juror in one labor trial and represented defendants in a sensational and nationally publicized murder trial.

In the movie, Spencer Tracy plays Henry Drummond, a fictionalized version of Clarence Darrow. Frederic March plays Matthew Harrison Brady, a fictionalized version of Bryan. Early in the trial, the judge narrowed the case to determine merely whether Scopes (called Bertram Cates in the movie and played by Dick York, of interest if you remember the 1960s and 1970s show *Bewitched*) had actually taught evolution in the classroom. And, indeed, he admitted he had.

But that didn't stop Darrow and Bryan from making the State of Tennessee vs. John Thomas Scopes into Faith vs. Science. Darrow/Drummond is a man who supports reason and intellect; the charismatic but physically declining Bryan/Brady defends the "truth" of the Bible.

In reality and in the film, Darrow asked Bryan a series of questions about the Bible, ultimately forcing Bryan to admit that at least some portions of the Bible are metaphorical, not literal.

Bryan conceded that some parts of the Bible were what he called "illustrative." That is, when the Bible calls the people "salt of the earth," it is not saying that they are literally salt. At that point, Bryan and fundamentalists lost in the court of public opinion, even though the judge found Scopes guilty of teaching evolution.

In the film, Bryan/Brady was clearly losing. He faltered, his voice lost its conviction and the crowd drifted away. He watched in bewilderment and then collapsed and died on the courtroom floor. Only his wife rushed to his side.

Bryan did die after the trial, but it was five days later.

The jury found Scopes guilty of teaching evolution, but the

judge fined Scopes a mere $100, and the Tennessee State Supreme Court threw the case out on a technicality a year later.

Bible literalists had won, but it was a Pyrrhic victory, and a very public one that had filled radio waves and made headlines across the nation. The whole trial had turned into a media circus; the town's merchants capitalized on its notoriety with a variety of monkey products, including "simian" ice cream.

As I watched the movie, I realized that Spencer Tracy's Drummond knows the Bible as well as Brady. There is a telling last exchange between Drummond and the hard-bitten, wise-cracking reporter covering the trial for *The Baltimore Sun*, modeled on the real-life H. L. Mencken. To the reporter's surprise — and mine — Drummond, mourning Brady as a once-great man, quoted a biblical passage.

HE THAT TROUBLETH *his own house shall inherit the wind: and the fool shall be servant to the wise of heart.*
(Proverbs 11:20)

THE POINT: This secular lawyer knew the Bible. He just didn't take it literally. There's such a difference. And it's a huge one. You don't have to believe the Bible is literal to use it as your guide.

There's another difference between the two opponents in *Inherit the Wind* and what we see today. And that is, although they vehemently disagreed with each other, they did respect each other. They truly were fighting over whether the Bible was to be taken literally. Today, the movement that is the great-great-grandchild of the Scopes trial is not about the Bible. It's about political power.

The "monkey trial" was a public relations fiasco for fundamentalist Christians, and they retreated from public life, stepping out of the limelight. Over the decades they created their own publishing houses and branched out into radio and television. Increasingly, they lived in an echo chamber of people like themselves — mostly white — and they embraced a credo of belief: To believe in God was more important than to be engaged in the world. It was easy to put on your car a bumper sticker that said: "Not of this world." Meaning, what you're working on is making sure that your faith matches what you need to believe in order to get into heaven. The focus is on the next world. Not this one.

In the 1960s, as ministers like Dr. Martin Luther King, Jr. led peaceful protests for civil rights, conservative evangelicals preached the opposite and questioned the motivations and patriotism of activist clergy. Mainstream Christian denominations, on the other hand, remained very much OF this world. They were open to others and their beliefs. They were diverse: white, Black, rural, urban, gay and straight. They embraced a wide breadth of causes; affordable housing, civil rights, immigrant rights, reproductive rights, LGBTQ rights and more. They tuned into a variety of media outlets; they didn't have a message that fit onto a bumper sticker. And their very openness to other ways of thinking meant that many of their children embraced the philosophy and morality of their parents' religions, but not necessarily the practice.

My family is the classic example. Of the six kids in my dad's family, only one of his five siblings married a Catholic. And only one of his five kids married a Catholic. In my case, it was not that I eschewed Catholicism. I'd really adored some nuns who were my teachers — the nun who taught me piano spent more time talking about liberal politics than teaching me my scales.When I was in college and in my 20s, I was crazy about Father Garthwaite's successor, Father Mark Walljasper. He was much different than Father Garthwaite. For one thing, he asked us to call him Father Mark, the first priest in my experience to do that.

Father Mark was a Democrat. He loved the Holy Father, as he called the pope. But when one of his parishioners proudly told him she'd voted for a Republican candidate because of his anti-abortion position, Father Mark snapped, "Shouldn't be a single-issue voter!" He was a social-justice-minded priest.

While I have great respect for a lot of Catholic priests and nuns working in the trenches, I'm a pretty stereotypical "none," meaning I'm one of those who checks "none," or "spiritual" in the religion box on questionnaires or online dating apps.

A lot of us nones have studied religion or were raised by churchgoers, we're into social justice, but we definitely do not wear our religion on our sleeves or tattooed on our arms. We're about social justice, about change right here on earth. But we don't go to church. And that makes us typical of many Americans.

As I mentioned earlier in this chapter, Americans are less religious than ever, with the "nones," those with no religious affiliation, increasing, White Christians were once the dominant Christian group in this country. They now account for less than half of the population. In 1976, 81 percent of Americans identified as white and Christian. In 2017, only 43 percent identify as white and Christian. The number of white evangelical protestants has dropped from 23 percent in 2006 to 17 percent in 2017. In the same time period, white Catholics fell from 16 percent to 11 percent and white mainline Protestants from 18 percent to 13 percent.One reason for that decline, according to Daniel Cox, PRRI's director of research, is that Christian activism is seen as conservative activism — opposing gay marriage, abortion and legalized marijuana. "It is no longer the case among young people that being religious is necessarily a positive attribute," Cox said.

There are a lot of reasons for religion's decline in the U.S. But the primary reason, I believe, is that the strongest and best-known Christian brand feels to me and a lot of other Americans as being against almost everyone except those who are white, straight, Christian and Republican.

---

1 History. https://www.history.com/this-day-in-history/castro-announces-mariel-boatlift

2 Lindner, John. "The Hundred Year Transition: From Protestant Privilege to Cultural Pluralism." *Reflections* https://reflections.yale.edu/article/how-firm-foundation-churches-face-future/hundred-year-transition-protestant-privilege

[3] Evans, Christopher H."How the social gospel movement explains the roots of today's religious left." *The Conversation.* July 17, 2017. https://theconversation.com/how-the-social-gospel-movement-explains-the-roots-of-todays-religious-left-78895

[4] Winston, Kimberly, "Christian America dwindling, including white evangelicals, study shows." *National Catholic Reporter.* September 6, 2017. https://www.ncronline.org/news/people/christian-america-dwindling-including-white-evangelicals-study-shows

3

A RACIST GOD

I had a friend who faced a terrible choice. She could deliver the fetus she was carrying, which would either be born dead or die shortly after birth. Or, she could have an abortion.

She and her husband chose abortion. A full-term pregnancy was an enormous physical risk for her. It was a straightforward decision for them. And it was hell.

"I wouldn't wish it on my worst enemy," she told me. She is a liberal Catholic.

I know women who carry genes for diseases that are fatal. Some have chosen to gamble and have the baby. Others have chosen abortion.

I had high school classmates who got pregnant. Some had abortions. Some chose to have their babies. Some married the fathers. Some gave their babies up for adoption. Some raised those babies on their own. Each made her own choice.

The important thing is: all of these women had a choice. I believe that all women should have the freedom to make that choice.

Sixty percent of Americans agree with me. Some want to limit the circumstances under which women can have an abortion, but they still believe in having a choice in many of those circumstances.

Religious conservatives used to have a very similar view about abortion. They didn't like it. But they didn't forbid it.

I shit you not.

As recently as the early 1970s,1 the Southern Baptist Convention discussed abortion and its basic decision was, "We don't like it, but it's a gray area, so let's just leave it. We've got more important work to do."[1]

In 1968, Bruce Waltke, an American Reformed evangelical professor of Old Testament and Hebrew, wrote that the Bible taught that life beings at birth. "God does not regard the fetus as a soul, no matter how far gestation has progressed. The Law plainly exacts: 'If a man kills any human life he will be put to death' (Lev. 24:17). But according to Exodus 21:22–24, the destruction of the fetus is not a capital offense... Clearly, then, in contrast to the mother, the fetus is not reckoned as a soul."[2]

In 1971, the Southern Baptist Convention passed a resolution affirming the need to protect women's access to abortion in the case of rape, incest and severe fetal deformity or if the pregnancy was to hurt the physical, emotional or mental health of the mother.

A famous 20th century fundamentalist wrote that he approved of Roe v. Wade, the 1973 U.S. Supreme Court decision that ensured a woman's right to choose to have an abortion. He was W. A. Criswell, former president of the Southern Baptist Convention and pastor of the First Baptist Church in Dallas, Texas.

"I have always felt that it was only after a child was born and had a life separate from its mother that it became an individual person," he wrote,[3] "and it has always, therefore, seemed to me that what is best for the mother and for the future should be allowed," he added.

The Southern Baptist Convention actually passed resolutions throughout the 1970s — in 1971, 1974 and 1976, the latter two after the 1973 Roe decision — saying that women should have access to abortions and that government should stay out of it.[4]

No one in the New Testament said abortion was wrong, wrote Garry Wills, author of more than fifty books on Catholicism. One of those books is called *Why I Am Catholic*. No one in the Old Testament said anything about abortion either, Willis wrote in an op ed in *The New York Times*. In 1930, Pope Pius XI forbade anything that prevented procreation, basing his edict on a flawed interpretation of a passage in the Bible. Scholars attacked his reasoning and the Vatican was so embarrassed that it never again tried to connect abortion with scripture. Now, the Church bases its anti-abortion stance on natural law, Willis wrote. He also pointed out that Catholic theologian Bernard Häring said that probably half of all fertilized eggs fail to attach to the uterus. Willis's wife had a high-risk pregnancy in the 1960s. Willis (clearly a worst-case scenario guy) went to the church for help in dealing with this scenario and found out that the church didn't suggest baptizing a miscarriage, or last rites or burying it in consecrated ground.

I'm a baby boomer. My parents and their friends had babies. Lots of babies. Sometimes one of our neighbors or an aunt would have a miscarriage. "Lose a baby," the adults said. As I grew up, my friends had miscarriages. Before I had my first daughter, I had a miscarriage.

In every instance, there was sorrow and sympathy.

But no funeral.

What happened? A 1970s court case.

No, it was not Roe v. Wade. It was a very different kind of court case that gave evangelical and political conservative leaders a way to light the fire under their evangelical voters. It was an ugly fire, the same kind of fire that burned the flaming crosses of the Ku Klux Klan. Abortion was merely an excuse that evangelical leaders used to disguise how they were tapping into latent racism among some of their rank and file to mobilize them and they could wave placards with gruesome images of mangled fetuses to quash any opposition. People who are evangelical and anti-abortion are not necessarily racist. But the origins of the movement they embrace so tightly are racist.[5]

A conservative political operative named Paul Weyrich, who was one of the founders of the Heritage Foundation, was the dark genius behind this movement. He and his associates claimed God was on their side. They built a gruesome PR campaign about abortion, catching the hearts of many. Weyrich and his strategists made abortion a black-and-white issue. Despite the distorted story much of the anti-abortion movement hypes, three quarters of Americans want Roe v. Wade upheld—but it is very nuanced. Some want more restrictions, some want fewer.[6] But the fact remains: they want it upheld.

Weyrich *welded* abortion to segregated schools trying to keep their tax-exempt status. Weyrich and his cronies wrapped the mantle of religion around abortion and then swept it around segregated white religious schools. No one was going to close these schools down—they could still segregate, they just couldn't get tax breaks if they did. The right made these schools' religious freedom the issue, denying that the issue was really about civil rights. And that thinly veiled racism dovetailed neatly with America's own, four-hundred-year-old tradition of racism.

It's something this nation has battled throughout much of its history.

In the early summer of 2020, the streets of America, from big cities to small towns like my little hometown in Wisconsin, filled with demonstrators, Black and white, protesting the murder of George Floyd and what his death represents. In August 2020, the streets filled again. This time it was because a police officer shot Jacob Blake, a Black man, in the back, in Kenosha, Wisconsin.

These demonstrations were a pushback against racism, which is as American as apple pie or the American flag. Witness the fact that the blatantly racist 1915 film *Birth of a Nation* was screened at the Woodrow Wilson White House. President Wilson, who won a Nobel Peace Prize for working to create the League of Nations, the predecessor to the United Nations, also wrote a history that praised the Confederacy and the KKK. He oversaw the segregation of many agencies in the U.S. government. Actions like this spurred Princeton University to remove his name from its public policy school. Wilson had studied, taught and finally served as president of Princeton.

The silent film was a landmark in moviemaking for its length, its use of techniques like fading in and out of scenes, a cast of hundreds and having a musical score. It was also a white supremacist film casting KKK members as heroes defending a society threatened by freed slaves portrayed as thugs who attacked defenseless white women.

Nor is racism a Republican phenomenon. The Republican Party was long the anti-slavery party, the party of Lincoln. Before the Civil War, Democrats in the North sided with anti-slavery Republicans. Some of those Democrats were in Wisconsin. Not just in big cities like Milwaukee and Madison, either. They were in rural Wisconsin. In places like Vernon County, which borders my home county of Monroe.

The Fugitive Slave Act of 1850 said that any runaway slave or suspected slave had to be returned to his or her so-called owners. But the state of Wisconsin declared the law unconstitutional and refused to take part. About 150 African Americans, many ex-slaves, formed one of the earliest and largest of these freedmen settlements, Cheyenne Valley in Vernon County, which lies south of my home county of Monroe. Among other things, they built distinctive round barns — which you still occasionally see — and may have opened the first integrated school in the nation.

Interestingly, Vernon County is on the bluer end of the purple spectrum in Wisconsin today. It's one of the twenty-three pivot counties in Wisconsin that voted for Obama in 2008 and 2012 and went for Donald Trump in 2016. But Trump just squeaked by in 2016 in Vernon County, with a 4.43 percent margin compared to Barack Obama's victory margins of 22 percent in 2008 and 14.73 percent in 2012. In Wisconsin's notorious pandemic election on April 7, 2020, Vernon County went for Jill Karofsky, a progressive Democratic-backed candidate, who handily beat Trump-backed Dan Kelly in a highly contentious state supreme court race that was officially nonpartisan but was in reality totally partisan. Trump carried Vernon County in 2020, but its Democratic congressional representative, Ron Kind, won reelection. No coattails there.

I include this historical footnote for two reasons. First, it's important to remember that although slavery is an American institution, there has long been a counterbalance. Opposing slavery is also an American tradition.

Second, we can't view this nation and its states and counties solely through today's headlines. We have to view today's events in their historical context.

The Civil War is with us still today, and its skirmishes will continue everywhere. It's in the streets of Kenosha, Madison, Milwaukee and other cities across the nation.

Here is where I see hope. These protests happened in new places, like the rural West and in small towns like my hometown. And, huge numbers of the demonstrators have been white.

Although there were slaves throughout the very young United States, the South was the cradle of that slavery, and

Southern Democrats were integral to slavery — and to institutionalizing racism in this country.

Southern Democrats were often slave-holding plantation owners, and it was Republicans who were the progressives when it came to the rights of African Americans. Southern Democrats were so powerful that after President Harry S. Truman, a Democrat, ordered integration for the military and other civil rights actions in 1948, Southern Democrats broke from the party. They were the Dixiecrats; they opposed the civil rights platform espoused by the Democrats and opposed federal regulations that they judged to be overriding states' rights.

Then came the 1954 U.S. Supreme Court decision, Brown v. Board of Education of Topeka (Kansas). It outlawed segregation in public schools. The South exploded. Mobs gathered, threatening the Little Rock Nine, meaning the African American students braving the storm to integrate classes at Little Rock Central High School in 1957.

President Dwight Eisenhower, a Republican, sent in the National Guard to hold back the mobs and enforce the Supreme Court ruling. The rule of law prevailed. But throughout the South, fury simmered.

The conservative National Review has written that as late as the 1960s, a higher proportion of Republicans supported civil rights legislation than Democrats. That said, a Democratic president, Lyndon B. Johnson, signed the Civil Rights Act of 1964, and it was Johnson's political genius that got that act passed. In contrast, his Republican opponent in the presidential race that year, Arizona Sen. Barry Goldwater, opposed the Civil Rights Act.

My point: When it comes to civil rights and Democrats and Republicans, nobody's clean. It all depends on what year you're talking about. Right now, Democrats are the party for African Americans. The Democratic Party is far from perfect, but today's

Republican voter suppression efforts hit people of color hardest. And Republicans have increasingly pumped Christian nationalism into their language and philosophy.

Racism has often used religion as an invisibility cloak in the United States. In fact, a Methodist minister, William J. Simmons, orchestrated the second coming of the Ku Klux Klan, in 1915, not long after the release of *Birth of a Nation*. He felt that the first iteration of the Klan had saved the South from racial equality right after the Civil War and he had a vision of a new incarnation of the KKK doing the same thing. His vision married white supremacy with Protestantism and America. The KKK targeted Catholics, Jews, immigrants and African Americans, groups Klansmen felt undermined a white and Protestant America. The crosses they burned were the symbol of Christianity. The cross on the Klan uniform included a teardrop symbolizing the blood of Jesus.

This does not mean American religions are racist per se. Not at all. American religions have long fought slavery and racism. In fact, early evangelicals were antislavery. In the nineteenth century, they sought to help those on the margins, according to Randall Balmer.

Balmer is a prize-winning historian, the John Phillips Professor of Religion at Dartmouth College and an Episcopalian priest. The latest of his more than a dozen books is *Bad Faith: Race and the Rise of the Religious Right*. His father was a minister in the Evangelical Free Church of America and that meant Balmer spent his childhood in different parts of the Midwest — Iowa, Minnesota and Nebraska. He went to Trinity College and Trinity Evangelical Divinity School.

In an interview with *Straight White American Jesus*, the excellent podcast hosted by Bradley Onishi and Dan Miller, which looks at the history of evangelicals, Balmer mourned what the religious tradition of his early life has come to represent.

Because evangelicalism today is very different from what it used to be.

Early evangelicals were part of antebellum prison reform efforts, peace crusades and the fight for women's equality.

Mainstream religions were also social justice advocates.

They were essential to change that marked the 1960s. Social justice minded churches were a major force supporting the Civil Rights Act after President John F. Kennedy introduced it in June 1963, just months before he was assassinated. Minnesota Sen. Hubert Humphrey, a Democrat, who supervised the bill's progress through the Senate, talked about the power of churches supporting the bill, saying that "they were the most important force at work."

The National Council of Churches (NCC), founded in 1950, became increasingly activist as the civil rights movement grew. National religious leaders started getting arrested at sit-ins protesting segregated public facilities in the South. Individual churches took a stand on racism.

To get the attention of national political leaders, the NCC formed a Commission on Race and Religion (NCC-CORR). Catholic and Jewish leaders supported them as the mouthpiece of the progressive religious social justice movement. They worked on two levels — lobbying leaders on the national level and getting the rank and file out of their pews and into the streets for events like the August 28, 1963, March on Washington.

If your Jesus is the guy who looks over the heads of the well dressed in the crowd to see what's happening to the folks on the margins and helping them, these religious leaders were doing the work of that Jesus.

Church leaders put themselves on the front lines. Dr. Martin Luther King, Jr., was one of the leaders of "Bloody Sunday," the March 7, 1965, voting rights march from Selma to Montgomery, the capital of Alabama.

A Racist God

Voting rights activists marched because Blacks made up about half of Selma's population, but only two percent had the right to vote despite ongoing efforts to register Black voters. Selma authorities used literacy tests and threatened violence to keep Blacks off voter rolls.

State troopers met the six hundred marchers as they approached Selma's Edmund Pettus Bridge, named after a Confederate general, US senator and grand wizard of the Ku Klux Klan. The troopers ordered the marchers, who were committed to nonviolence, to stop. The marchers stood their ground. News clips of the day show troopers pushing against the marchers, shoving them to the ground and mounted police galloping toward the people on the bridge. Smoke from tear gas clouds the screen. The 2014 film *Selma* portrays graphic images of bludgeoning, beating and violence. The late Rep. John Lewis, who represented Georgia's fifth congressional district from 1986 until his death in 2020, was among the marchers. Then just twenty-five, he was one of the leaders. Police clubbed him so viciously that they fractured his skull.

Two days later, white men with clubs attacked three Unitarian ministers who were participating in the demonstrations. One, the Rev. James Reeb, a Unitarian Universalist minister from Boston, died from his injuries, giving his life for civil rights.

Much of the nation was horrified and outraged by these days of blood and violence.

Not the Rev. Jerry Falwell.

Two weeks after the march, he gave a sermon titled "Ministers and Marches" criticizing such activism. "Preachers are not called to be marchers," he said, "but soul winners."[7]

He then tried to cast doubt on the motives of Dr. King and other leaders of the march. "I do question the sincerity and nonviolent intentions of some civil rights leaders such as Dr.

Marting Luther King, Jr, Mr. James Farmer and others, who are known to have left-wing associations," Falwell said.

Falwell and evangelical theologians like Francis Schaeffer were scared not just about people of color asserting their rights, but by a general undermining of the America they wanted, which was white, straight and Protestant. And they saw plenty to be upset about.

In 1962, the US Supreme Court ruled in Engel v. Vitale that it was unconstitutional for state school officials to create a state school prayer and push to have it recited.

As the conflict in Vietnam intensified, Americans sat in their living rooms and kitchens and watched young soldiers carry their dead and dying comrades out of the jungles and rice paddies of Vietnam. (Another historical footnote; early in the war, Blacks made up 11 percent of the fighting force but accounted for over 20 percent of casualties. Black leaders protested. President Johnson cut back Black participation in combat units, and the percentage of Black casualties fell to 11.5 percent by 1969). Anti-war protests, student sit-ins and demonstrations dominated the headlines.

One night in 1970, anti-war activists blew up a lab at the University of Wisconsin in Madison because the US Army partially funded it. They did not realize that grad students were working in there. The explosion killed one student and injured several others. That same year, National Guardsmen shot and killed four demonstrators at Kent State University in Ohio. I was in high school then. Many of my classmates felt the students deserved to be shot. "But they weren't armed!" I said. That changed some minds.

Riots raged in inner cities from Newark, New Jersey, to Watts in Los Angeles. Thirty-five states ratified the Equal Rights Amendment, which was designed to ensure the rights of women but which religious and social conservatives considered a threat to the family. It fell short of the required thirty-eight states, but it was close.

In 1969, homosexuals fought back when police raided the Stonewall Inn, a popular gay bar in Greenwich Village, giving birth to the gay rights movement

Rock and roll reigned, with anthems decrying the war and police brutality while celebrating sex. The theologian Francis Schaeffer wrote about his fears that all of this resulted from secular humanism campaigns designed to undermine both morals and America's Christian roots.

Something, these religious conservatives believed, had to be done to turn all of this around. Evangelicals were perfect. They were already organized, homogenous and a white constituency. They were a minority, yes, but they were a big minority that could tip the scales in Republicans' favor. Plus, a lot of those evangelicals were in the South, a newly vulnerable Democratic bastion, thanks to the Democratic Party's embrace of civil rights and Nixon's so-called "southern strategy" for the GOP. Southern voters were reeling from the challenges to nearly a century of racist Jim Crow dominance. They were doing end runs around civil rights laws and, when it came to keeping white students and Black students apart, religious fundamentalism was the perfect shield.

Soon after Brown v. Board of Education in 1954, white students began to disappear from public schools in the South. In one year in Holmes County, Mississippi, the number of white students in public schools plummeted from more than 700 to 28. The next year, that number hit zero. Where did those white students go? The answer: religious segregation academies, tax-exempt religious schools.

This didn't happen only in Mississippi. It happened all over the South. Jerry Falwell, Jr., the Rev. Falwell's son, had his own segregation academy in Lynchburg, Virginia.

Then came that catalytic court case, Green v. Connally. All those segregation academies had enjoyed tax-exempt status. But Green v. Connally, rendered in 1972, ended that benefit. The US District Court for the District of Columbia ruled that any institution that practices racial discrimination or segregation is not tax exempt. That decision mobilized a lot of these preachers who had just lost a key way to separate white students from Black students.[8]

It lit the fire that mobilized all of those apolitical evangelicals. But, of course, they couldn't overtly campaign on a "Keep Our Schools White" slogan. It had to be about the state impinging on their religious freedom.

Paul Weyrich, who had co-founded The Heritage Foundation, had been eyeing evangelicals. He, too, saw their potential as a political force that could give the Republican Party an immense advantage in the polls. He saw opportunity in Green v. Connolly. Weyrich positioned the elimination of tax-exempt status of segregated religious schools as government coming down harshly and unfairly on religious institutions. He cast it as an impingement on freedom of religion to Southern evangelicals, who would give the Republican Party just what it needed to crush the Democrats in the South, and, as it turned out, in other parts of the nation as well.[9]

Abortion also held potential, Weyrich and others seeking to harness the power of evangelical voters realized. Anti-abortion groups seemed to help Republicans defeat Democrats in Indiana, Iowa and South Dakota in the late 1970s.

The historian Randall Balmer has immersed himself in Weyrich's papers, traveling to Wyoming to read Weyrich's writings at the University of Wyoming American Heritage Center. Balmer, interviewed on NPR, said that as he read Weyrich's writing he could feel Weyrich's excitement leaping off the page as he realized abortion could rally the troops. Abortion might have been the catalyst, but protecting segregation was the goal. I'm not saying abortion opponents are racist. I'm saying they were hoodwinked.

And then, in 1980, along came Ronald Reagan.

At first glance, Reagan seemed like an unlikely champion for the religious right. He was divorced, had actually signed the most liberal abortion law in the nation while he was governor of California and was a product of the Hollywood moviemaking machine that evangelicals often decried as the source of so much that was undermining America's Christian roots. On top of this, he was running against America's first evangelical president.

President Jimmy Carter was that rare Democrat who talked about Jesus easily. He talked about reading the Bible every day. Carter taught Sunday school, for goodness' sake! He was opposed to abortion, but was far less extreme than the anti-abortion movement of today. He supported the Equal Rights Amendment, which, as noted, many conservatives saw as an attack on the family because they believed it would undermine traditional gender roles.

Carter, elected in 1976, was a progressive evangelical. Hard as it is to believe today, there was a progressive evangelical movement. In fact, on Thanksgiving weekend of 1973, fifty-five evangelical leaders produced The Chicago Declaration of Evangelical Social Concern. This was a manifesto that reflected evangelicalism's historic roots opposing slavery and lamenting the gap between rich and poor. The Chicago Declaration decried racial and economic inequality, it stood up for women's rights and it criticized the nation's militarism. Carter, as governor of Georgia, was in sync with this group, but much of this was the antithesis of the conservative social agenda the religious right was putting together.

President Carter lost to Ronald Reagan in a landslide in 1980.

The economy was tepid. The country suffered from "stagflation," a trifecta of low economic growth, high inflation and high unemployment. And, the nation faced a series of energy crises. Gas prices soared. The Iranian hostage crisis, in which 52 American diplomats were held hostage for 444 days in Teheran, dragged on and stayed in the headlines. Democrats bickered, Republicans united. Reagan focused on the Communist threat and fighting big government.

It worked. The religious right probably was not essential to Reagan's victory. But it was definitely a factor. Reagan's victory encouraged the leaders of the religious right — and Republicans who were more than willing to brand their party as the party of God — to ramp up a far more sophisticated operation that in 1984 made the religious right a political force to be reckoned with.

And what this movement focused on was power and strength. Nothing about the meek inheriting the earth. Anywhere.

---

[1] ALLEN, Bob. "Southern Baptist Convention's abortion stance moving toward birth control issues." *Baptist News Global* March 5, 2014 https://baptistnews.com/article/southern-baptist-convention-s-abortion-stance-moving-toward-birth-control-issues/#.YF3gAWRKirc

[2] Dudley, Jonathan. "When evangelicals were pro-choice." CNN.com. October 30, 2012. https://religion.blogs.cnn.com/2012/10/30/my-take-when-evangelicals-were-pro-choice/

[3] Hargrove, Brantley. "The Late First Baptist Dallas Pastor W.A. Criswell Was Pro-Choice." *D Magazine*. May 29, 2014. https://www.dmagazine.com/frontburner/2014/05/the-late-first-baptist-dallas-pastor-w-a-criswell-was-pro-choice/

[4] Allen, Bob. "Southern Baptist Convention's abortion stance moving toward birth control issues." *Baptist News Global* March 5, 2014 https://baptistnews.com/article/southern-baptist-convention-s-abortion-stance-moving-toward-birth-control-issues/#.YF3gAWRKirc

[5] Blumenthal, Max. "Agent of Intolerance," *The Nation,* May 16, 2007. https://www.thenation.com/article/archive/agent-intolerance/

[6] Montanaro, Domenico. "Poll: Majority Want to Keep Abortion Legal, But They Also Want Restrictions." NPR. June 7, 2019. https://www.npr.org/2019/06/07/730183531/poll-majority-want-to-keep-abortion-legal-but-they-also-want-restrictions

[7] PBS, "People and Ideas." https://www.pbs.org/wgbh/pages/frontline/godinamerica/people/jerry-falwell.html

[8] Balmer, Randall. "The Real Origins of the Religious Right." *Politico Magazine,* May 27, 2014l https://www.politico.com/magazine/story/2014/05/religious-right-real-origins-107133/

[9] Balmer, Randall. "The Real Origins of the Religious Right." *Politico Magazine,* May 27, 2014l https://www.politico.com/magazine/story/2014/05/religious-right-real-origins-107133/

4

TRUMP THE MESSIAH: CHRISTIAN NATIONALISM

I understand disdaining meekness.

The Jesus Christ on the cover of the catechism book I used as a kid had long, sun-streaked brown hair and blue eyes looking meekly heavenward from under his eyelashes. A bunch of adoring lambs and blond children sat at his feet. I thought this entire scene was too tiresome for words.

It was so, well, holy. Suffer, put up with it and pray.

It probably didn't help that my Uncle Zel had created an act of fake holiness that he used to bother all his nieces and nephews.

He'd walk into our library, which was the TV room for us kids but which my mother called the library. He'd stand in front of the TV, blocking our view, and clap his hands together in prayer and look heavenward with, I swear to God, the exact same expression of the Christ on my catechism book. "Holy, Holy Uncle Zel," he'd intone, "He will never go to hell."

This drove us crazy. In those pre-Cartoon Network days, we could only watch cartoons on Saturdays, and only until 10 a.m., when my mother would kick the five of us out of the house.

"Uncle Zel," we'd holler, "Move!"

"I'm praying," he'd say sanctimoniously, still looking skyward, pretending to be so focused on prayer that he could not hear us. I never saw anyone so unctuous until Ted Cruz came on the scene decades later.

It made us mad as hell because we were too little to push him out of the way (although we'd try).

Uncle Zel was the first grownup I'd ever heard make fun of the wimpy Jesus.

It turns out that Uncle Zel (who went to church every week — although he'd slip out right after Communion just as the priest said "to love and serve the Lord") and I were not the only ones who thought that Christ was often portrayed as a wuss.

Kristen Kobes du Mez, author of *Jesus and John Wayne: How White Evangelicals Corrupted a Faith and Fractured a Nation*, explains that a lot of Christians, who, unlike Uncle Zel and me, actually read the Bible, also felt that Jesus was too wimpy. They've replaced that wussy Christianity with a way more muscular one.

The Jesus in my catechism took care of the poor, the sick, the weak. Mary Magdalene was presented as a prostitute and he treated her with respect. If you're going to be Christ-like, you have to be for all of those outsiders, That means making sure everyone has good healthcare even though your opponents call good healthcare socialist. (My definition of socialism: capitalism with a heart). It means cleaning up the environment and creating good jobs in the process. It means everyone can get a good education. It means making sure everyone feels valued for who and what they are. It's about love and respect.

That is not the language of the religious right. For the religious right, Christ-like means aligning with a muscular, gender-based he-man Christianity of the conquering hero.

The movie *Braveheart*, popular viewing for many evangelical youth programs, epitomizes this kind of Christianity. It stars a virile Mel Gibson whose character fights impossible odds for his country, an oppressed Scotland, and family. It's full of blood, sex and intrigue.

This hyper-masculine Christianity posits that men are warrior-hunters while women wait passively at home for them. Muscular Christians view themselves as part of a nation that has to be armed and ready for an attack by the godless, and any sign of mercy is weakness.

With that as context, it's easier to understand why President Trump's belligerence so resonates with lovers of he-man Christianity. (Not that he looks anything like a buff Mel Gibson in *Braveheart*.)

When Trump said to the governors of a nation roiled by antiracism protests, "If you don't dominate, you're wasting your time. They're going to run over you. You're going to look like a bunch of jerks. You have to dominate," he was singing to a very specific choir.

He continued to build on that message to a group that tries to justify tactics of violence and intimidation by invoking God's name.

On January 6, 2021, a mob of Trump supporters, many of them armed and some carrying zip-tie handcuffs they intended to use on members of Congress, stormed the US Capitol building. Among the banners they carried: flags declaring "Jesus Saves" and "Jesus 2020." At the rally rioters attended before they stormed the Capitol, Rudy Giuliani, Trump's attorney, called for "trial by combat."

The Pentagon called the riot an act of "sedition and insurrection" in a memo to active duty and reserve troops. It also told the troops that it was their duty to protect and defend the Constitution against all enemies, "foreign and domestic." Even Mitch McConnell, while still the Senate majority leader, blamed Trump for the violence, saying the mob had been "fed lies" and "provoked by the president." The insurrection was part of a Trumpian pattern, most dramatically illustrated in June 2020. That's when riot police used tear gas to clear peaceful protestors out of Lafayette Square across from the White House so Trump could wave a Bible for the cameras in front of St. John's Church. The bishop of the Episcopal Diocese of Washington, Mariann E. Budde, denounced the move.

Trump and his supporters have interwoven the Republican Party and Christian nationalism. The conspiracy group QAnon (now an FBI-designated terrorism threat) has interwoven Christianity into its platform. QAnon postulates that it supports Trump and his battle against a global conspiracy of pedophiles. This is a lie. (I should not have to say that but in this era I do).

A few Christian leaders have been pushing back on Christian nationalism for years. There were a few deathbed conversions in the wake of the January 6 terrorist assault on the Capitol, when attackers evoked God and Jesus, with "Jesus Saves" and "Jesus 2020" banners, Confederate flags and crosses. This linking of white supremacist and Christian symbols and rhetoric gave some Christian leaders pause. After the attack on the Capitol, faith leaders were nearly unanimous in condemning what Robert P. Jones, CEO of the Public Religion Research Institute called an "unholy amalgamation of white supremacy and Christianity."

But the fact remains that there were clergy participating in the riot and some had helped to publicize the event.

The notion of a muscular Christianity is not new. Just look at the Crusades. This was ostensibly a series of wars between Christians and Muslims over control of holy sites that both considered sacred. But on a political level, it was Western Europe flexing its muscles and gaining power for European Christians over the Holy Land and more.

He-man Christianity raised its head again in the mid-1800s

in England when clergyman and author Charles Kingsley wrote the book *Two Years Ago*.[1] It equated being a strong and healthy man with being Christian and worked on getting boys to man up.

In the United States, also in the 1800s, the educator and physician William Alcott wrote extensively about physicality and religion. Alcott made a vegetarian diet and exercise integral to Christianity. He also included moral improvement, a duty to God and meeting your responsibilities to family, contemporaries and posterity. A father had to be robust to provide for his family, Alcott wrote. His book, *The Young Man's Guide*, is still available.

William Alcott's second cousin, Amos Bronson Alcott (the father of author Louisa May Alcott), was a health nut, too — he was vegan (although the term didn't yet exist). His take on Christianity also married physical and moral fitness — but combined that with support for abolition and women's rights. This Alcott was an innovative educator who started several schools (one failed after he admitted a Black student).

Probably the best American example of muscular Christianity was Theodore Roosevelt, the 26th President of the United States. He was president from 1901 to 1909. Roosevelt was a sickly child, asthmatic, skinny and bullied as a teenager. He was determined to recreate himself and did so by committing himself to a physically demanding lifestyle.

Victorian masculinity felt threatened by industrialization and innovations in psychology and physiology[7]. Sounds familiar, huh? Roosevelt himself challenged "effeminacy of character," and "WASP malaise" with working out and immersing himself into an outdoor lifestyle.[2]

Roosevelt accomplished a lot. He was a war hero, built our national defense system, was an outsized conservationist who protected approximately 230 million acres of public land, was a trust buster who fought big business and sparked outrage by inviting Booker T. Washington, the Black educator and orator, to the White House. A lot of what he did looks pretty liberal today in the context of that era. That didn't mean he was secular. When in the heat of battle, he did not hesitate to invoke God. "We stand at Armageddon and battle for the Lord," he said at the 1912 Republican Convention.

Now, let's go back to the creation of this great nation and compare nineteenth and early twentieth century rhetoric with the writings and beliefs of our founding fathers.

They were students of the Enlightenment, the seventeenth century movement that focused on reason and individualism over tradition. It drew on the thinking and writings of philosophers like Rene Descartes, John Locke and Isaac Newton, not the Holy Bible. Also, philosophers like Immanuel Kant, long seen as secular; Voltaire, a critic of Christianity and the Catholic Church, and Jean-Jacques Rousseau, who was not anti-religion, but realized that religion could be seen as something that competes with the state.

The very first clause in the US Bill of Rights, known as the Establishment Clause, states that "Congress shall make no law respecting an establishment of religion."

This clause has long been interpreted as separating church and state. In 1802, President Thomas Jefferson wrote that the Establishment Clause built a "wall of separation between the church and the state."

But we've seen continuing efforts to ride roughshod over our founding fathers intent to keep church and state separate. Instead, the right has tried to more deeply embed Christian sensibilities into the American story. That effort went into high gear in the 1950s.

If you take a look back at our recent history, it's easy to see that President Donald Trump, standard bearer of the Christian right, was not an aberration. He was the culmination of seventy years of hard work by people who have devoted themselves to using their version of Christianity to meld the Republican Party into what it is today, a Christian nationalist party whose goal is to cement its hold on a demographically and culturally pluralistic nation. Christian nationalists are a shrinking minority; they know it. It's what makes them so desperately afraid and angry. They know they have to do all they can to hang onto their power. And they have to do it *now*, or they'll be out of time. It's why they were so focused on voter suppression in the 2020 election. And it's why Republican legislatures are industriously passing even more aggressive anti-voter laws today. As an example, Georgia's new laws, which, besides ramping up identification requirements for absentee ballots and limiting ballot drop boxes, make the act of giving water to voters waiting in line in the hot Georgia sun illegal.

What would Jesus say to *that*?

Fewer voters in an increasingly racially and culturally diverse country make it easier for Christian nationalists to win elections. This is something that Paul Weyrich, seen as the architect behind a mobilized anti-abortion movement, knew very well. He once admitted that "our leverage in the elections quite candidly goes up as the voting populous goes down."[3]

Christian nationalists believe that to be American means you have to be Christian. For many, it also means you have to be white. Let me make clear, being Christian does not mean you are racist. Far from it. But many leaders of the right are pushing racist policies — voter suppression is just one.

The Rev. Billy Graham laid the groundwork in the 1950s for what's happening today when he wove patriotism and Christianity together. After Martin Luther King's 1963 "Letter From a Birmingham Jail," Graham said King should "put the brakes on a little bit." Graham focused on the Second Coming. He didn't think the federal government could right systemic injustice; he criticized civil rights leaders for trying to change laws instead of hearts and didn't believe government could fix things. Only Jesus's Second Coming could. So for him, it was all about belief,[14] faith and the apocalypse.

Graham began gaining fame in the early days of America's Cold War with the Soviet Union. It was an era of proxy wars, spies and fears of traitors from within. This was the McCarthy era, so named for Wisconsin Sen. Joe McCarthy. It was a time of red baiting and of blacklisting of government officials, academics and writers. Graham cast the geopolitics of the day in Biblical term. "I believe today that the battle is between communism and Christianity," he said in a speech quoted in historian Frank Lambert's "God in America."[4] Graham's rhetoric wasn't democracy v. communism. It was that of a God-fearing America facing down the godless Communists.

Graham even counseled President Eisenhower — who had never been baptized — about becoming Presbyterian. Don't mistake this for a big conversion. Eisenhower had been raised in a deeply religious family, and faith was important to him. His parents were members of a church that was an offshoot of the Mennonite faith. They were very devout — Eisenhower's father read the Bible to the family every night — but Mennonites (along with a lot of other religions) don't baptize infants, they wait until they are older and presumably have a better understanding of the significance of baptism. Eisenhower was not formally part of any faith; he rectified this at age sixty-two after he became president. He was baptized at the National Presbyterian Church in Washington, D.C., the church his wife Mamie belonged to.

Eisenhower, too, made faith part of the fight against communism. His inaugural address opened with a prayer he wrote himself. He started his cabinet meetings with a moment of silent prayer. That was something of a reflection of the times. Church membership rose from 49 percent of Americans in 1940 to 69 percent in 1960.[5]

Eisenhower believed religious faith distinguished American democracy from Communist oppression. It was part of the American arsenal in the Cold War. Evangelicals were comfortable with him.

Evangelicals lost their man in the White House with the 1960 election of John F. Kennedy, a Catholic. JFK defeated Richard Nixon, who had been Eisenhower's vice president, in a very close election.

Evangelicals feared President Kennedy could be an agent of the pope. Kennedy addressed this suspicion head on by making a speech that said he believed in the separation of church and state, as laid out by our founders.

"I believe in an America where the separation of church and state is absolute, where no Catholic prelate would tell the president — should he be Catholic — how to act, and no Protestant minister would tell his parishioners for whom to vote, where no church or church school is granted any public funds or political preference, and where no man is denied public office merely because his religion differs from the president who might appoint him, or the people who might elect him."[6]

Fighting words, huh? Imagine how that would go down today with evangelicals and some priests. Many of them would call him a godless socialist!

And so thought the evangelicals of the 1960s. They had some work to do. The Rev. Jerry Falwell was just the guy to do it. He took the foundations the Rev. Billy Graham laid in the 50s and 60s and carried them to new heights in the 1970s. Falwell's overall theme: America was blessed but was straying from its Christian foundations. Falwell and his followers ignored the roots of the Constitution and continued building the myth of a Christian state. Yes, most Americans were Christian, but they were not citizens of a Christian state. I was in college at the time, at the University of Wisconsin-Madison. The lakeside campus was packed with liberal Democrats like me. But one of my dormitory mates, politically moderate, that year became a born-again Christian. She'd party with us liberal sinners but then haul her hung-over ass out of bed on Saturday mornings to attend prayer meetings with some of the (not-hung-over) neighbors in our dorm.

They were part of the Praise the Lord, or PTL Club, whose origins lay with the ultimately disgraced televangelist couple, Tammy Faye and Jim Bakker. The Bakkers were part of Pat Robertson's Christian Broadcasting Network. Tammy Faye, who was famous for her garish makeup (I actually loved that because I felt you could never wear too much eye makeup) and her husband Jim built an empire that finally came crashing down in the 1980s amidst of a series of financial and sex scandals. Jim Bakker and Jessica Hahn, the church's twenty-one-year-old secretary, had a sexual encounter in 1980. She called it rape, he called it consensual.

That scandal broke seven years later, in 1987, along with the financial scandal. Bakker was convicted of twenty-four counts of fraud and ultimately spent five years in prison. The trial focused on $165 million in donations. He now hawks food for survivalists preparing for the end times.

In my view, then and now, he was a cheater. The twin scandals only heightened my suspicions of televangelists and my belief that they were hypocritical hucksters. Tammy Faye stood by her man publicly, but finally divorced him in 1992, saying that she was done "pretending that everything was all right."

Looking back now, as a woman who for far too long also told only the good parts about her marriage, all I can say is "Amen, Tammy."

When my dorm mate was dragging herself to those PTL

meetings, James Dobson's first book, *Dare to Discipline* was published. Dobson is a pediatric psychologist whose organization, Focus on the Family, helped to define the political right's family values.[7]

In subsequent books, Dobson emphasized traditional gender roles, with men being creatures of action, while their women waiting for them. Similarly minded authors followed. One was Steve Farrar, who wrote the 2003 book, *Point Man: How a Man Can Lead His Family*. Point man? A point man is the lead soldier on an infantry patrol in combat. Right. The implication: The family is a combat unit in a new holy war.

Dobson and other influencers wove their version of God into the nation's political, economic and social policy. He-man Christians had to stand against the feminists who they saw as undermining the evangelical family structure — and, implicit in this, emasculating men.

All of this was happening as Jimmy Carter, a born-again Christian, was elected president in 1976. He epitomized progressive evangelicalism, words that today seem mutually exclusive. President Carter fought poverty and supported racial equality and human rights in general. He signed the Equal Rights Amendment in 1978, meant to ensure equal rights for women, before it was forwarded to the states for ratification; the political right saw and sees the amendment as bound to undermine the traditional American family. The amendment still is not part of the Constitution.

Carter, the progressive evangelical, epitomized much of what the nascent Christian right feared and hated.

This progressive evangelicalism and its focus on the world we live in as opposed to beliefs that will get you into the next clashed with the socially conservative agenda espoused by Jim Bakker, Jerry Falwell and their followers.

So rather than support Carter, these conservative evangelicals turned to a former Hollywood denizen — and former governor, Ronald Reagan. Throughout the 1970s Reagan had come down on the Soviet Union; national defense was a major theme for him. Further, picking up — either deliberately or coincidentally — on Graham and Falwell's theme, Reagan cast the United States as God's country. With these talking points, Reagan fit in perfectly with an explicit Republican strategy aimed at courting southerners dissatisfied with the Democratic Party — ironically because of Jimmy Carter, their fellow Southern evangelical in the White House. In essence, Reagan was catering to the nationalistic tropes of the emerging religious right.

Looking back, I think that this is where the Republican Party sold its soul to the religious right in return for the power this bloc's votes would give Republicans.

Some Republicans fought this effort to merge the religious right and the Republican Party. Senator Goldwater, who failed to unseat President Johnson in 1964, was one of them. In that year, Goldwater was a member of the conservative wing of the Republican Party and did not have the full-throated support of moderate Republicans, led by Nelson Rockefeller (governor of New York from 1958 to 1973). Johnson won with a definitive 61 percent of the vote.

Goldwater, who represented Arizona in the US Senate from 1953 to 1965 and again from 1969 to 1987, was very different from conservatives of today. He warned about the dangers of the religious right.

"I'm frankly sick and tired of the political preachers across this country telling me as a citizen that if I want to be a moral person, I must believe in 'A,' 'B,' 'C' and 'D,'" he said in 1981 in interviews and in a speech on the Senate floor.[8]

He made a key point about the dangers of infusing affairs of state with religion. In a speech in the Senate, he told Americans to "look at the carnage in Iran, the bloodshed in Northern Ireland or the bombs bursting in Lebanon." He blamed this violence on "injecting religious issues into the affairs of state."

By separating church and state, Goldwater said, America had spared its citizens the kind of intolerance that has divided the world with religious wars. Funny how the increasing polarization of our country has paralleled the growth of religiously driven politicians and their loyal followers.

When televangelist Jerry Falwell opposed the appointment of the first woman to the US Supreme Court, Goldwater said: "I think every good Christian ought to kick Falwell right in the ass." That nominee, Sandra Day O'Connor, served on the Court from 1981 to 2006.

Goldwater criticized "moneymaking ventures by fellows like Pat Robertson and others [in the Republican Party] who are trying to... make a religious organization out of it."He lobbied for homosexuals to be able to serve openly in the military, supported abortion rights[32] and the legalization of medical marijuana.

Goldwater stood up to the religious right. He criticized its efforts to mold the Republican Party in its image. But his was a voice in the wilderness in the Republican Party.

As the Republican Party became one and the same with the religious right, it also took on the thinly disguised racism of Christian nationalism.

Trump's own racism and misogyny are a match with the racism and misogyny of many evangelicals, according to Nancy D. Wadsworth, associate professor of political science at the University of Denver, author of *Ambivalent Miracles: Evangelicals and the Politics of Racial Healing* and co-editor of *Faith and Race in American Political Life*. White evangelical Protestants feel besieged by cultural change and, Wadsworth says, racism and intolerance are more woven into the fabric of evangelicalism than most Christians want to admit.

To be evangelical does not mean you are racist. But Trump's "Make America Great Again" slogan hearkens back to an America that institutionalized racism, a racism that, if you were white, you probably didn't notice. And while I am sure a lot of Trump supporters and other Republican voters can honestly say they never used the "n" word and were never consciously sexist, the guy they voted for was trying to bring back a world dominated by whites and men. Evangelicals and conservative Republicans who voted for Trump and vote for and cheer the Republican politicians and legislators who continue to champion Trump's agenda (shutting our borders, making it harder to vote, making abortion illegal and denying science) have sold their proverbial souls in exchange for power and dominance.

But guess what. They're still afraid.

Randall Balmer, the prize-winning historian raised as an evangelical, says, with great sadness, that evangelicals have lost their moral compass.

"Any time racism is not addressed, it festers," he said in an interview on the podcast, *Straight White American Jesus*, which focuses on the religious right and its impact on politics and culture.

"Over the decades it became a bleeding wound, and we saw the results of that in the outcome of the 2016 election," he said. "I don't know how anyone can argue that there is an entity called evangelicals any longer. It seems to me that it died in 2016 after a long, lingering illness that began in 1980."

Balmer is in mourning for a once-admirable movement. "In an earlier era of American history, it really stood for some remarkable principles. Look at nineteenth century evangelicals; they were always arguing for those on the margins," he said. They were involved in the anti-slavery movement in the North, prison reform in the antebellum period, peace crusades and equality for women.

"Overall evangelicals in the nineteenth century looked out for those on the margins, those Jesus called the least of these," he said. When you compare 19th century evangelicals with the religious right of today, Balmer added, "you find almost no correlation."

I believe that this morphing of evangelicalism into Christian nationalism is a movement based in fear. Fear of the other. Fear of the new. Fear of change. Fear of the future.

And, as we learned all too well on January 6, 2021, fear makes today's evangelicals very dangerous.

---

[1] BUCK, Stephanie. "When Jesus got too 'feminine,' white dudes invented Muscular Christianity." Timeline. January 19, 2017. https://timeline.com/muscular-christianity-20d7c88839b9

[2] Christen, Gordon J. "Roosevelt, Boy Scouts and the Formation of Muscular Christian Character." Macalester College, Religious Studies Department. April 24, 2014. https://www.macalester.edu/religiousstudies/wp-content/uploads/sites/42/2016/10/Gordon_Christen_2014_Thesis.pdf

[3] Billmoyers.com Team. "The Shadow Network." October 21, 2020. https://billmoyers.com/story/new-podcast-the-shadow-network/

[4] Butler, Anthea, "How Billy Graham weaponized white evangelical Christian power in America." MSNBC. May 19, 2021. https://www.msnbc.com/opinion/how-billy-graham-weaponized-white-evangelical-christian-power-america-n1267874

[5] Hitchcock, William I. "How Dwight Eisenhower Found God in the White House." History.com. August 22. 2018. https://

www.history.com/news/eisenhower-billy-graham-religion-in-god-we-trust

[6] Wolraich, Michael. "Why evangelicals love Santorum, hated JFK." CNN. March 1, 2012. https://www.cnn.com/2012/03/01/opinion/wolraich-catholics-protestants/index.html

[7] McAfee, James. "James Dobson and the American Right: Interdiscursivity and the construction of rhetorical agency." Iowa State University Digital Repository. 2013. https://lib.dr.iastate.edu/cgi/viewcontent.cgi?article=4416&context=etd

[8] Broder, David S. "Goldwater Lashes Religious Pressure." *The Washington Post.* September 16, 1981. https://www.washingtonpost.com/archive/politics/1981/09/16/goldwater-lashes-religious-pressure/b1caa379-49fa-4e04-82de-dccda6f5e7f9/

5

JESUS IS MY VACCINE

My friend Skip Frazee spent summers in high school mowing the lawn and trimming the grass from around the gravestones at Woodlawn Cemetery on the eastern edge of my hometown of Sparta, Wisconsin.

One day, he noticed a row of gravestones indicating that four or five members of the same family had died within weeks of each other in 1918. He pointed it out to one of the older crew members, Skinny Scaife.

"Oh," said Skinny, who'd been about six years old in 1918, "that was the year of the Spanish flu pandemic."

That was Skip's introduction to pandemics.

Skip and I have remained friends; I see him and his family a lot on my frequent visits home. When he and I talked about those graves in May 2020, while Covid-19 ravaged the nation and the world, I realized how much a cemetery can tell you.

Woodlawn is a pretty cemetery on a hilly knoll overlooking Sparta's middle school and beyond that, homes, fields and tree-covered hills. Gentle breezes often tickle the trees when my kids and I visit my dad's grave and those of my Aunt Liz and Uncle

Allan; my aunt and uncle who were like a second set of grandparents for my girls.

Very near my dad's grave are the graves of other relatives. One reads "Thomas James Rice, son of John D. and Mildred Rice. July 2-Aug. 11, 1949." And then, beneath that: "Polio Victim." That baby was the fourth child of my dad's oldest brother, John D., and his wife, Millie.

Aunt Millie, tall and slender with white blond hair, had the Nordic beauty of Frances Farmer, the 1940s movie star immortalized in the 1982 film, *Frances*. Aunt Millie spoke only Norwegian until she was five, and for much of her early life, she lived in small Norwegian communities. As a teenager, she loved dancing and she and her younger sister Enva went to dances, wearing party dresses Millie had made herself. She graduated from high school at sixteen and then earned a bachelor's degree in education at what is now the University of Wisconsin-Eau Claire. Her first teaching job was in Sparta; she was so drop-dead gorgeous that my Uncle Zel came home and told his dad about the stunningly beautiful new math teacher. Her beauty did not mean her students behaved, though.

The twenty-year-old teacher had a class full of football players just a little younger than she was. They totally ignored her as a teacher, frustrating her so much that she almost quit during her first week there. But her mother told her she had a choice — she could either leave or she could show those recalcitrant boys who was boss. She stood up to those boys and taught for several years. And she didn't just teach. She brought her love of dance to Sparta, organizing the first junior prom Sparta ever had.

Uncle John D. had a little Frank Sinatra in him. He almost always sported a bow tie with his Brooks Brothers suit and tilted his driving cap at a rakish angle. He ran WCOW, the Sparta radio station his mother (my grandmother) owned. He was a charming troublemaker, the kind of guy who would set off firecrackers in his mother's bedroom at dawn every Fourth of July, jump out of her bedroom window onto the adjacent sleeping porch, tip his hat at whatever startled boyfriend or girlfriend of one of his five younger siblings might be sleeping there, and scamper off.

"Oh," my grandmother would chuckle indulgently at breakfast. "That's my oldest son, John D. He does that every year."

He'd bounced around working as a reporter at newspapers from Wisconsin to California, and eventually returned home to run WCOW. As a reporter, he held everyone's feet to the fire — city council, county board and school board. WCOW blared in every barn in the county, country music during the day, news at seven in the morning, noon and five at night. It wasn't just news. He would also broadcast his editorials about particularly contentious local issues, clearly and fearlessly taking his position.

"I didn't always agree with him," said one farmer I knew after he died. "But I always listened."

Uncle John D. golfed, drank martinis on the rocks and smoked Pall Malls or Tareyton cigarettes. He played piano at every party he ever attended. And if he was there, it was a party, and he was at its center. He had his own little Rat Pack, all World War II vets like him who'd come back home to Sparta to raise their families and the occasional bit of hell.

John D. and Millie met just as World War II loomed. John D. had just returned to Sparta from working as a reporter for the *Wisconsin State Journal* in Madison. A reporter at the LaCrosse Tribune set him up on a blind date with Millie, a woman who could manage a classroom full of recalcitrant football players, plan a dance party and make the perfect dress for it.

Their marriage-bound courtship was a race against time. He was going to war, and he and Millie knew it. They married in the fall of 1943, with Millie ignoring her Norwegian Lutheran mother's protests about her daughter marrying a Roman Catholic. Eventually, Millie's family came to adore John D. But her mother did not attend their wedding.

When their son Mike and I tried to figure out the timeline of their early life together, we could not believe how they packed in all that they did.

I see Aunt Millie as Uncle John D.'s Angie Dickinson, the exquisitely pretty actress who played Frank Sinatra's exasperated wife in the original *Ocean's 11* and also ran with the Rat Pack. In their wedding photo, Aunt Millie is slim and beautiful in a satin and lace confection of a wedding dress that she designed and sewed herself ("It has I don't know how many buttons down the back," my cousin Christy remembered); Uncle John D. is dapper in a uniform that fit so well he must have had it tailored. They look as glamorous as any Hollywood couple of their era. And also, a little wide-eyed. There was a lot going on.

They went off to war, together, with Aunt Millie accompanying her new husband to Texas, where he was first stationed. There she had one baby. That baby, tragically, died. Years later, when St. Mary's Hospital in Sparta got a respirator for preemies, Aunt Millie said to her daughter, "If we had had that twenty-five years ago, that baby would have lived." She promptly got pregnant again, then John D. was shipped off to Alaska (family lore has it that he almost shot down a plane carrying New York Mayor Fiorello La Guardia). Millie and her new baby, my cousin Mike, returned to Sparta to live with her parents-in-law.

When the war ended, John D. came back, and it seemed as if they then had a chance to take a few deep breaths and really begin their lives together. They had another son, my cousin Dubbie. And in 1949, they had another.

Nineteen forty-nine was one of the worst polio years ever. The polio virus thrived in summer. It hit everyone, but it was particularly vicious in the way it targeted children. Those under five were the most vulnerable. Across the nation, cities closed movie theaters, churches, swimming pools, even swimming holes. Preachers broadcast church services over the radio. And still the virus, spread mostly by air droplets, raged.

Thomas James Rice was one of its victims.

When he died, Millie had a nervous breakdown.

"It destroyed her," my cousin Christy, the daughter Millie had a few years after Tom's death, told me.

The mental health professionals of the 1950s used the tools they had at hand for my Aunt Millie, who endured things like electroconvulsive therapy, an often-stigmatized treatment that can be helpful and is still used today. While she recuperated, her two young sons, Mike and his younger brother Dubbie, lived with my grandparents for nearly a year. It was a busy house. An Eastern European couple from a displaced persons camp in eastern Europe, Otto and Irma, moved in with my grandparents shortly after Mike and Dubbie showed up. Mike remembers that Otto and Irma doted on him and his brother. My Aunt Pat, her husband and kids lived next door and were in and out all the time.

By the time I came along, Aunt Millie was back in action. Our families did a lot together. I can remember loving going to dinners at their house, my sister, brothers and I playing in Christy's backyard playhouse, where flowers wound around its casement windows. Aunt Millie had turned an old chicken coop into a playhouse. While we played, the adults hung out in the kitchen or by the grill.

Our two families would go on picnics and fishing expeditions on Sixty Acres, a stretch of land on the LaCrosse River that my grandmother owned. My dad and his brothers played together so much that for a few years, my parents, Aunt Millie and Uncle John D., and my Uncle Zel shared a cottage. Eventually, my parents, figuring that with five kids they needed their own place, bought another cottage just up the road from the first one. Once they had things like driver's licenses, the bigger kids played with us less and a cottage held less appeal for them. But Aunt Millie's kitchen in town stayed full. It's where her kids and their friends always ended up.

She had a rich life mothering her children and their friends. But it was not nearly the life she could have had. The consequences of Tom's death during that brutal summer of polio might fade into the background for years, but they could come roaring back, dogging Aunt Millie and her family. Life beyond her home, husband and kids could sometimes be hard for her to manage. Rice family gatherings were always loud and rambunctious, with political debates and singing around the piano. I loved it! In fact, family get-togethers where guests sit in one place and stay there, take turns talking, never interrupt and don't have a piano, make me really nervous. But it can be hard to marry into my boisterous family and I think it was even harder for my Aunt Millie as years wore on. Eventually, she just would not be around. And somewhere in the back of my mostly oblivious child's mind, I knew exactly why.

I tell this family tragedy to show that when a pandemic rips through a society, its victims extend far beyond those who got sick and those who died. There's a ripple effect that goes on and on and on, reverberating through families and through the years.

In 1955, only six years after Tom's death, a polio vaccine developed by Dr. Jonas Salk became almost universally available. And in Sparta schools, there was a clear line that illustrated its efficacy. In classes of kids born in the early 1950s or earlier, there were students in wheelchairs or on crutches. And, of course, graves. After 1955: none. There was one exception, a girl in a wheelchair who had been born after the vaccine became available and was a few years younger than I.

"Her mother didn't bother to have her vaccinated," my father said once, with a rare flash of anger.

Everyone else in her class had gotten vaccinated.

They all walked.

She never did.

When I was in grade school in the 1960s, we kids would line up in the school gym at Lakeview Elementary (prosaically named because it overlooked Perch Lake) to get our polio booster shots every year. We were so happy when they upgraded to a liquid served in a small paper cup that you could down like a shot.

Everyone believed in vaccines back then.

I still do.

I was living in New York City when the pandemic hit in March 2020. That April, sirens screamed so constantly in the city that one of my neighbors told me she felt as though she were living through the London Blitz. I believe in social distancing, facemasks and the efficacy of soap and water in dissolving the gel that encapsulates the virus, rendering it harmless.

At the same time those sirens were screaming in New York, hordes of demonstrators, some armed, most crowding closely together without facemasks, were storming the Michigan state capitol. Most were pandemic skeptics who argued the nation had succumbed to unjustified hysteria. Some even put signs on their trucks and cars.

"Jesus is my vaccine."

Science and faith have long had a rocky relationship.

"Conservative Christianity has always feared science," Colby Martin told me. He is a former evangelical pastor who is now co-pastor of a church, Sojourn Grace, that affirms the LGBTQ community, is egalitarian in its theology and practice and embraces diversity — in race, gender, sexual orientation, socioeconomic status, physical ability, age and more.

Colby pointed to the fact the Catholic Church in 1663 found the Italian astronomer Galileo guilty of heresy when he said the earth revolved around the sun. It was more than three hundred years before the church officially acknowledged that Galileo was right and cleared him of heresy.[1]

The religious right has carried on that same science-denying tradition. This goes back to the Scopes trial, which pitted science against a literal interpretation of the Bible. If you're a Bible literalist, evolution says the Bible is wrong, that God did not create the world in six days, that he did not create Adam and then Eve. Evolution, according to this worldview, blows up the biblical creation story and is the first step down a slippery slope that leads to atheism.

That's one reason the religious right rejects science. But rejection of science is not limited to the religious right. It's part of the broader political right's identity as well.

I saw hordes of other Covid doubters in August 2020 after I dropped my younger daughter off for her freshman year of college in Ohio. I was so relieved that she was able to go to college in person rather than remotely that I didn't get the empty nester blues I'd worried about. But I didn't want to go back to my apartment in New York either. It was too full of ghosts and tears. On top of that, it was on the market and an encouraging number of potential buyers were streaming through it (observing tight Covid protocols, of course). I wanted to stay out of my real estate agent's way.

So I had decided to keep heading west. First, I stopped in Wisconsin, staying in my family's cottage in Monroe County for a few days. Then, I pointed my car west, planning stops in Park City, Utah, which was at that point easing some Covid restrictions, and then Cortez, Colorado. Short-term, at least, I was a gypsy. And I dug it.

I hit South Dakota at the height of the Sturgis Motorcycle Rally. Motorcyclists surrounded my little Subaru Crosstrek (stick-shift, of course; I grew up in a gear-head town). I passed campground after campground filled with attendees and I felt a little comradeship with them.

I've been a motorcycle rider. I even had a Harley once. My dad actually bought it for us kids! To my mother's fury. Only three of us five kids were old enough to ride it at the time. My sister was obsessed with the rider lawnmower (no surprise she married a golf course superintendent), and my sixteen-year-old brother was usually in trouble and not allowed to use it. So it was essentially mine. I'd ride it to my job as a bartender at the Officer's Club at nearby Fort McCoy, reveling in the way you could feel changes in the temperature as you rode from one microclimate to another. I loved the way you could feel the speed in a way unequaled by anything I ever experienced until, decades later, when I flew in the Concorde, the supersonic jet.

Operated by British Airways and Air France, the Concorde traveled at twice the speed of sound. It cut the flight between New York and London from five or six hours to three hours. I once flew aboard the Concorde from London back to New York. As the plane's acceleration pressed me into my seat, I looked down at the curve of the earth and then to the seat back in front of me, watching the speedometer move to Mach 2. It immediately reminded me of 130-mile-an-hour motorcycle rides on moonlit nights along Monroe County's hilly back roads with one of my boyfriends. So, when those motorcyclists roared by me near Sturgis, wind whipping their hair, I understood the appeal.

There's a little outlaw aspect to being a motorcycle rider. In fact, the motorcycle world has a downright raunchy side. A high school classmate attended a Sturgis rally several years ago and

Jesus Is My Vaccine 77

came home with stories of "bushiest beaver" and "big titty" contests.

Sturgis fans and Bible believers might not seem to have much in common. But they do. The contests my classmate saw advertised are a tiny part of Sturgis — it also includes biker ministries. As I drove along with my biker escort in the summer of 2020, I thought about other similarities between Sturgis attendees and conservative Christians. When I looked at news photos of the events in Sturgis, I saw only a few facemasks on the crowded streets. Leading the South Dakota Covid deniers: the state's governor and Trump loyalist, Kristi Noem, She spent $5 million on "South Dakota Is Open for Adventure" travel ads when Covid experts were pleading with Americans to stay home, invited Americans to Sturgis and called Covid a Democratic plot to take over the country.[1]

The first time I drove past Sturgis, South Dakota's Covid numbers were low. But a month later, South Dakota's Covid cases had quadrupled and the CDC was calling the state one of the most dangerous in the nation. In September I left Colorado and drove east back to Wisconsin, where I planned to work as a volunteer for Monroe County Democrats during the 2020 election. (Yes, my urban Democratic friends, there are Democrats, lots of them, in farm country!) I drove through South Dakota again. I was listening to NPR as I drove and it reported that Covid numbers were dropping in many parts of the nation, but increasing in South and North Dakota. When I checked into my hotel in Rapid City, South Dakota, I was the only person in sight wearing a mask. Not even the hotel clerks of the Country Inn & Suites I stayed in wore them. When I got to my room, Fox News was playing on the TV. When I checked out the next morning, I turned on CNN. If the hotel staff left that TV on CNN, subsequent guests would eventually have learned that Sturgis, which attracted 460,000 people to its 2020 rally, was a super spreader event that spawned an estimated 260,000 Covid cases.

A few weeks later, Noem hit the campaign trail for President Trump, stopping in Sparta on October 1, to stump for Trump at the Monroe County Republican Party headquarters. By then, South Dakota's Covid cases had quadrupled. I was back in Monroe County at that point. I just shook my head when I heard about Governor Noem's visit. Then I resumed making phone calls to make sure Democratic voters in Monroe County knew where they could vote and how, and drove around dropping off Biden-Harris signs for Democrats in little villages, at farmhouses and in housing developments where a lot of military veterans lived, thanks to the proximity of Fort McCoy and the Tomah VA hospital. Wearing a mask and keeping my distance, of course.

Noem likes to play up her cowgirl roots — she grew up on her family's ranch and quit college to help run it after her father died in a farm machinery accident. That rugged individualism resonates with people in Monroe County and with Americans in general. I get it.

I love the idea of the cowboy and cowgirl culture and the freedom it represents. This is one reason I have a fabulous and totally impractical cowgirl fringed leather jacket. I think American individualism is one of our nation's strengths. But, we have to recognize that freedom must be tempered by the fact that our actions can hurt others. Every time we obey a stop sign or traffic light, we acknowledge that our freedom is limited by its impact on others.

Overall, though, as a nation, we are less committed to collective action than a lot of other countries, according to Naomi Oreskes, a professor of the history of science at Harvard University. Oreskes believes that when Trump supporters like Noem (who got vaccinated in April 2021, early in the game) and others like her reject the efficacy of masks or the reality of Covid, they are not really anti-science. They talk and behave the way they do because they don't like what those policies imply. She calls this implicatory denial and usually they don't like these policies because they conflict with their worldview, which emphasizes the importance of individual rights. I also think that they just can't bring themselves to agree to *anything* proposed by anyone who is not a far right winger. They are just that contrarian. All an irresponsible president and his sycophants had to do was characterize facemasks as an impingement on their freedom, and presto, the anti-mask movement was born.

Creating anti-maskers was made easier because of the belief that less government is better, a belief that Ronald Reagan posited so effectively that even Democrats like President Bill Clinton echoed it. Again, unscrupulous leaders cast masks — seen as effective in curbing the flu pandemic a century ago — as big government crushing our freedom.

Now, less government is a highly subjective concept. For the far right, big government, I think, is a dog whistle for its undefined bogeyman socialism. Which in turn is code for godless communism. Monroe County is really red. But do you know how much in farm subsidies its farmers pocketed between 1995 and 2020? More than $88 million dollars.[2] Some might call farm subsidies socialism, because they were designed to give farmers some protection from the ups and downs caused by weather, commodity pricing, the economy and crises like, well, pandemics. Do these subsidies limit farmers' freedom? I don't think so! It's a classic example of what I call capitalism with a heart.

Move from the scientifically proven efficacy of masks and vaccines to scientifically proven climate change and you get another focus for science denial — climate change. When I was traveling through the Midwest and West in the summer and fall of 2020, I encountered a lot of extreme weather that was obviously the result of climate change. One August night in Monroe County, a thunderstorm raged for hours, dumping five to nine inches of water onto fields, roads and streams. The next morning, I squeezed in a run between storm cells and discovered that a section of the road I always run on had washed out.

A milk truck lay in the ditch near the washout. Fortunately, the driver, who'd been making his usual pre-dawn run to pick up milk, was fine. A Monroe County Sheriff Department officer on the scene promptly eased my concerns on that. He also told me radar showed another storm was en route. I turned around and headed home.

The Monroe County Highway Department went right to work fixing the road. The next morning I picked my way around the washed-out section of road and saw that crews had brought in a new culvert and piles of sand. Weather isn't climate but I couldn't help noticing the new culvert was twice the size of the rusted-out culvert it was replacing.

This happened at the same time that Hurricane Laura threatened to obliterate Houston. I worried about that because one of my cousins and her family live there. Laura was a fearsome storm because it drew its powerful, 150-mile-an-hour winds from 90-degree water. Had Laura hit Houston head on, it might have destroyed much of the city. Laura's power peaked the same time that thunderstorm dumped buckets of water on Monroe County.

When I was in Cortez in southwest Colorado over Labor Day 2020, visiting my brother and sister-in-law, I'd go on my run early, before the day got too hot. An orange-pink veil of smoke from California wildfires hung in the sky. The smoke cloaked the entire West. One brother was in Reno, and the smoke made him sick. The smoke cloud dropped ashes on the streets of

Whitefish, Montana, where my daughter and her friends were living, forcing outdoor lovers to stay inside, windows closed.

Scientists say the forest fires that now threaten areas of the country long impervious to forest fires burn thanks to conditions created by climate change. They blame climate change on the rising temperatures of oceans, which then generate more powerful hurricanes. Ditto for the increasingly extreme thunderstorms that pound the Midwest and other parts of the country.

Fighting climate change would seem to be something the Bible tells you to do — we're supposed to be good stewards of the earth that God created. But the religious right and the political right cannot accept climate change. The biggest reason, I believe, is that it would mean they agree with their opponents: the secular, the liberal (and to the right, I think a moderate looks liberal). However, they can't say that. So instead, politically powerful religious groups are doing their best to defend their stance by casting environmentalism and climate change as a false worldview.

One such group is Focus on the Family, a fundamentalist Christian organization dating back to 1977 that promotes politically conservative public policy. It does acknowledge that God wants Christians to be good stewards of the earth. But, the group also falsely says environmentalists are what it calls pro-abortionists pushing abortion [3] because they're worried about over population, which is a lie. It's another example of how the religious right welds its abortion fight to unrelated issues.

Another group the Cornwall Alliance, says it's for preserving the beauty of earth for the glory of God. But it calls concerns about global warming over blown and warns that it's really about going down the slippery slope of socialism, the favorite amorphous and undefined bogeyman the right uses to demonize Democrats.[4]

There's a perverse beauty to these undermining efforts to save our earth. Even when the religious right acknowledges climate change, there's a backup argument for letting it happen. Because, Jesus will clean it up.

It's all about the apocalypse. It comes and wipes out everything and then Jesus shows up and makes everything neat and clean again. (When I heard that one I thought, *There has got to be some smarty-pants evangelical kid who told his mom he didn't have to clean up his room because the apocalypse is coming and Jesus will clean up said room along with the rest of the world.*)

Climate change, according to this interpretation, could actually be a sign of the approach of the end times.[5]

For a lot of evangelicals, accepting that climate change is real means more than denying the truth of the Bible. For also means you are allying yourself with the very people you have been taught for years are trying to undermine America's Christian roots.

Denying climate change is not about religion. It's about race and politics. Social scientist Dan Kahan, a professor at Yale Law School and former faculty member at Harvard Law School and the University of Chicago Law School, explains it this way.

He says religion is not the main predictor of your attitude about climate change. A better predictor is your race and your political philosophy. He says if you are white and politically conservative, you're more likely to reject climate change and science.

Proof of this: Conservative white evangelicals generally deny climate change. In contrast, Black evangelicals accept that the climate is changing. A sign of hope for those of us who would like to save this earth: climate change denial could become a problem for the religious right and the right overall. Here's why: according to a 2014 PRRI survey, nearly a third of evangelicals acknowledge that the climate is changing.

There is an evangelical environmental movement that believes what I think the Bible tells us. And that is that the environment is God's creation, so taking care of the environment is the Christian thing to do. It's also got a social justice element — pollution hurts the poor the most.

Creation Care is a group arising out of the evangelical environmental movement. It believes God made us stewards of the earth. The fact that climate change intensifies world poverty is important to this group. Another Christian environmentalist group promotes political activism; Interfaith Power and Light calls on Christians to lobby Congress and lays out other actions the religious can take to fight climate change. IPL reported in November 2019 that 770 congregations across the nation use solar power — they call this "Energy from Heaven."

In other words, evangelicalism is facing a split in the ranks when it comes to the climate. Yes, a substantial proportion of evangelicals and other conservatives continue to deny climate change, but there's that chunk of them who believe it is happening. The latter group is part of the two-thirds of Americans who accept climate change but also believe the federal government is not doing enough to fight it.

This group: millennial evangelicals. Born between 1981 and 1996, they are more in favor of stronger laws to protect the environment than older evangelicals.

They differ from their parents in other ways — they are more likely to say that immigration is good for the United States. These younger evangelicals, unlike their elders, favor bigger government providing more services to people.

Millennial evangelicals give me hope. They are our future. And I don't think they will grow out of it. Because there are older evangelicals who believe strongly in some of the same things these younger evangelicals believe in. For instance: being pro-immigrant and pro-refugee. I think that one of Jesus's most powerful messages — and I am looking at him as a historical figure, not as God — was his focus on the other, the little guy, the outsider, the leper. All along, there have been evangelicals who have done just that: opened their arms to welcome those whom I think are today's "other," the people outside the camp, whom Jesus reached out to. These modern-day others are refugees and immigrants.

The National Association of Evangelicals (NAE) has been very vocal about its belief that America should support refugees. Galen Carey, vice president of government relations for the NAE, testified before Congress in February 2017, calling the U.S. refugee resettlement program the "crown jewel of American humanitarianism."[6]

Carey's is a voice of quiet reason. It's one you didn't hear amplified on Fox News and you won't hear on any of the new conservative sites like Newsmax. We don't expect evangelicals to champion refugees and immigrants, and that makes it hard for many of us to hear what Carey has to say. It doesn't fit our image of evangelical Christianity because the zealots drown him out. But once you can get around the deafening noise of Christian nationalists, you'll find a lot of Christians like Carey. They take out full-page ads in places like *The New York Times*. They organize into groups like The Faith and Policy Initiative at American Progress.

This is a group that uses faith in a way that makes sense to me, with a focus on clean air and water, creating good jobs, addressing economic inequality and fighting for racial justice, reproductive justice, religious liberty, LGBTQ equality and immigration reform. Its main goal: freedom for all. To me, they sound pretty damn American.

No question, conservative white evangelicals are a big minority that remains strong and united. And it is really, really loud. It tunes in to the right's own cable propaganda machine,

Fox News. Fox may be losing credibility with this group but conservative propaganda is hydra-like. Lose one megaphone and two more pop up in its place.

In the wake of the 2020 election, this minority is building new media networks (like Parlor), which will continue to silo the Christian right. That means this group will continue to live in its own reality, one that truly believes Trump won the election and that Covid-19 is a myth, that climate change is an effort by Democrats to take over the nation and that immigrants and refugees put us in danger..

As to the trickle of defectors, I don't expect that to turn into a torrent, but they remain important. The mainstream media tends to focus on the fact that Trump won vast majority of religious voters but pays little to no attention to the fact that he lost a chunk of these voters to Joe Biden in 2020. And Trump's loss of religious voters was Joe Biden's gain.[6] That's news worth investigating. Fostering the doubts among these evangelicals are evangelical leaders who are doing some intense soul searching. One example: Ed Stetzer, head of the Billy Graham Center at Wheaton College in Illinois, calling on his fellow evangelicals to look at how they might have helped fuel the January 6, 2021, armed assault on the U.S. Capitol that saw domestic terrorists come within seconds of taking members of Congress hostage.

This emerging group shows that there is a chance to work the margins, to collaborate with Christians unafraid to stand with the broad-minded and generous-hearted. And there is one more issue that could be an Achilles' heel for white evangelicals.

Homosexuality.

---

[1] RODRICK, Stephen. "The Covid Queen of South Dakota." *Rolling Stone*. March 16, 2021. https://www.rollingstone.com/

politics/politics-features/south-dakota-kristi-noem-covid-1142068/

[2] Environmental Working Group Farm Subsidy Database https://farm.ewg.org/top_recips.php?fips=55081&progcode=totalfarm&regionname=MonroeCounty,Wisconsin

[3] Focus on the Family. 2011. https://www.focusonthefamily.com/family-qa/christians-and-the-environment/

[4] Schlanger, Zoe. "The 'scientists' who support Trump's choice to run the EPA are creationists with opaque funding sources." *Quartz*. 2016. https://qz.com/888424/a-climate-denying-evangelical-group-connected-to-the-koch-brothers-supports-trumps-choice-to-run-the-epa/

[5] Morris, Alex. "Donald Trump: The End Times President." Rolling Stone. October 30, 2020. https://www.rollingstone.com/politics/politics-features/donald-trump-christians-fundamentalists-end-times-rapture-1083131/

[6] Carey, Galen, Vice President of the National Association of Evangelicals, remarks to the US House of Representatives, February 2, 2017. https://www.nae.org/responding-current-refugee-crisis/

[7] Orr, Gabby. "How Biden Swung the Religious Vote." *Politico*. November 11, 2020. https://www.politico.com/news/2020/11/11/how-biden-swung-the-religious-vote-435954

6

TRUE LOVE: GAY CHRISTIANS

David Lloyd is one of my best friends from childhood. His family and my family both owned cottages on the same pond in Wisconsin. It's a magical place called Spring Bank, a turn-of-the-last century Midwestern Shangri-La. Tall pine trees tower over a pond lined with simple one-story cottages and a log cabin. It's full of Victorian follies like a swinging bridge, a Witch's cave, rock-sculpture water fountains spraying water into the air and ornate little stone bridges arcing over Sparta Creek, which runs through Spring Bank.

Summer after summer, David and I, his sisters, my brothers and my sister and kids from other cottages on the pond all played together, swimming in the pond, having water fights in canoes and going hiking in the woods. We read books on the raft, fought over Monopoly games on rainy days and made up stories about us as adventurers when we wandered the woods.

We all wintered in different towns and states, but every summer we'd pick up where we'd left off the previous fall. Then, when David was eleven or twelve, his family left Spring Bank. David's parents, a doctor and a nurse, became medical missionaries and the entire family went off to Madagascar. They were medical do-gooders in the name of God. Faith, religion and God are still what drives their lives.

It was a monumental move. It surprised me, because I had never thought of them as being particularly religious. But they chose to practice their profession as health care providers to serve God and spread his message of love.

And David, their only son, is gay. He is one of the most exuberant people I know and I love him for it. When he walks out of the cottage to greet the morning, he throws his arms wide open to the skies to embrace the day. He is a high end travel concierge—as you might expect of a kid who spent his adolescence in Madagascar and was then sent off to boarding school in Paris. He knows exactly when the sunlight shining into St. Mark's Basilica in Venice is at its most exquisite and can make sure you are in there at the moment—without crowds of other people to distract you. Need a helipad last minute in Turkey? He'll get it built for you—and he has. Not for me, but for someone else. He is a big-hearted soul who believes in God. He has a wicked side-eye that allows him to make the most straight arrow remark seem deliciously naughty.

Dr. and Mrs. Lloyd were good-humored but quite earnest people. I could never figure out how a pleasant but decidedly sober couple like them had had a son like David.

I cannot imagine what it was like to grow up a golden gay boy in a rural area where wrestling and football ruled. Then, on top of that, to find yourself transplanted to the world of missionaries off the east coast of Africa.

David's parents returned to Spring Bank after working as medical missionaries for several years. They jumped into similar work in west central Wisconsin, with Habitat for Humanity, food drives, and even building houses for bats at Spring Bank to maintain their habitats.

Dr. Lloyd died several years ago, with David at his side.

David and I often see each other when our visits home overlap; he'd come from Chicago and I'd come from New York.

And in March in 2020, when I bailed out of New York after a meteor called Covid-19 hit New York City and hauled my daughter and her dog to Spring Bank, I called up David and asked him what it was like to be a boy like he once was.

He remembered his father's missionary friends meeting him and seeing their knowing looks that some of them gave him. No one was ever overtly unkind, but he could see how some would dismiss him as a legitimate person because of his flamboyant, exuberant nature-because he was gay.

At the same time, he told me when we talked about what being gay was like for him, he would encounter people who he called truly Christlike. These were people capable of unconditional love, who did not judge him for his personality or sexual preference but loved him just as they loved any child of God.

These were people who embraced a god of loving kindness, not a vengeful god who threatened eternal damnation because of who you loved.

Christians who embrace a god of love rather than a god of vengeance are raising their heads increasingly in the religious world. It's hard to hear a message of love when so much vitriol is being spouted in the name of Jesus. But try to see if you can hear it. I did. And I found the message of a loving God in a lot of places. One of the most memorable was at the Wild Goose Festival in July 2019. There, I saw women walking around wearing "Free Mom Hugs" t-shirts. This is a group of parents and their allies who love the LGBTQ community unconditionally. Their goal is to educate families, churches and civic leaders to affirm and celebrate the LGBTQ community. And part of that is the very simple act of hugging; hugging their own children— and other people's gay children.

Sara Cunningham, a Christian mom who had to struggle to

embrace her own son's sexuality after denying it for much of his life, founded Free Mom Hugs.

Cunningham is from Oklahoma City and she is a woman who has made a pretty incredible journey, one from a church that excludes people to a world that embraces gay children like her own son.

She is a mother who had found a home for herself and her family in an evangelical church. She remains respectful of all that it provided her and her husband and children for 20 some years.

She had two sons and early on could see how different they were. One was rambunctious and outgoing; the other was quiet and liked to play with girls. At five, he came downstairs wearing one of her dresses and a pair of her heels. A kid who loves to play dress up in his mom's clothing is not necessarily gay. But Parker was gay, and his mother refused to admit the truth to herself. Finally, when he was twenty-one, he forced her to face reality. He came to her and told her he had met someone, and that someone was a man. She could not deny it any longer. She had to face the reality of having a gay son. Sara found herself in a foreign territory.

She had bought into her church's teaching that to be gay was to be damned. She feared for her son's eternal soul and she also feared for his safety right here on earth. The only gay men she could think of were Liberace, Elton John and Matthew Shepard, the gay college student at the University of Wyoming who was brutally beaten and left to die near Laramie.

She dealt with it by immersing herself in her son's world. Then she wrote and self-published a book about it: *How We Sleep at Night: A Mother's Memoir*. It is the story of her journey from church pews to gay pride parades.

She went to her first gay pride parade in Oklahoma City. And she hugged everyone. She would first ask—because not everyone is a hugger. And then she hugged. She would not let go until they let go. That first year, she came home from the parade covered in glitter.

She kept reading and talking and learning. The more she learned, the more shocked she became. She heard about parents who turned their backs on their children. Gay people who found themselves without a home to go to, abandoned by their families, abandoned by their churches. Abandoned by their faith, a faith that told them God's love was conditional. That they had to change who they were to be accepted by God.

Cunningham is forthright in admitting her regrets and her mistakes in handling her son's sexual identity. That's one reason why her message resonates with women who once were mothers in denial and then in despair about their children. She and Free Mom Hugs hit the road, so that women like her, women who loved their gay children but felt so alone, would learn that they were NOT alone. And, of course, it wasn't just mothers. It was fathers, too.

Cunningham and her group did a road trip from Oklahoma City to the Stonewall Inn in New York City. They then did a second, one that went to the Matthew Shepherd memorial.

The group stopped in cities at spots that welcomed them, coffee shops, libraries, "anywhere folks would listen and share our stories."

They met mothers everywhere who felt the same way Cunningham had felt when she faced reality. They, too, had thought they were the only ones in, say, Topeka, Kansas, who had a child who was gay. In every town, those mothers met other mothers just like them.

When she found that some gay couples had parents who would not attend their weddings, she took action.

She put up a post on Facebook telling anyone who was gay whose biological parents refused to attend their weddings, that she would attend in their stead, and she offered to bring the bubbly.

It went viral. Among those who saw it: the actress Jamie Lee Curtis. She saw the post, discovered Cunningham's book, and called her up.

The story of Sara Cunningham and her son Parker is going to be a movie on the Lifetime channel.

Last April, as Covid seemed to suck all the air out of the world, I saw something else on Facebook. It, too, was about love. It was the marriage of two friends I'd made at the Wild Goose Festival, Kathy Hopson and Jes Miller. The two women had been planning their marriage when I met them in the summer of 2019.

Jes had been raised Catholic but found a home in a Pentecostal church. She still misses all that revivalist energy. But it was a world that required her to deny a key part of herself, her sexuality.

At sixteen, she tried confiding in her mother and it devastated her mother. She filled their home with holy water, palm fronds, a huge photo of Jesus and scenes from the Bible.

Jes retreated "I was like, 'Oh, mom, I was just kidding.'"

Then a crisis hit when Jes was eighteen. Her closest friend from her hometown was killed in a car accident. By that time, Jes had a girlfriend. They had met at Pentecostal Bible camp; the girlfriend joined Jes at the funeral. Their relationship was clear to the associate pastor.

The day after the funeral, he pulled Jes aside. "You've got to get right or you've got to get out."

She had been very involved with the church, running a youth group. She had been four-wheeling at the associate pastor's home with his kids just two weeks earlier.

Some might say she chose to leave the church. But Jes didn't see it that way. She was gay, and the church was unyielding. Her mother couldn't understand why Jes was suddenly not doing anything with her church.

"I said, 'Because I lied to you when I was sixteen. I'm gay,'" Jes told her.

Jes and her mother today are very close. But it was rough there for a while. Today, Kathy's photo has joined the photos on Jes's mother's wall. Both of Jes's grandmothers adore Kathy.

But for several years, religion had no part in Jes's life.

The rejection was profound for her. She was angry with it.

Then she met Kathy; a mutual friend set them up on a date and they became a couple.

Jes was still done with religion, but she saw how important it was to Kathy. They'd spend a weekend together and Kathy would leave Jes to go to church.

"I wanted to see what this was all about," Jes said, but she was not up for being rejected yet again by religion. But, "I saw God working through Kathy," she says. "I had to go to the church that was filling her up in such a wonderful way."

Kathy was raised in the United Methodist Church; she went to church every Sunday with her parents and her sister. She described her father as conservative and her mother as liberal. Kathy was deeply involved in her church,was president of the youth group and did Bible study classes, just as Jes had been involved in hers. She found a church in college and was the youth counselor. She spent ten years in that church and even married a man. The marriage lasted nine months.

"That didn't work, for obvious reasons," she said.

She was still at that Methodist church, but there was no one her age in it. She'd go to a service with 85 people and she was the only person her age there, by at least 20 years. So she went shopping for a new church. This landed her at a big evangelical, fundamentalist church. A thousand people would attend services there every Sunday.

"I loved the social aspect of it," She taught Sunday school and was part of a women's Bible study group. Kathy spent two years there and gradually began noticing things she found discomfiting. For one thing, "There were no women in ministry," she said.

"They don't tell you up front," she said about the limits placed on roles women could play in the congregation, "They draw you in and then you find out," she explained.

A woman in her early 20s who was in the Bible study class played guitar and was very outgoing.

"Someone said, 'You should become the next worship leader,'" Kathy remembered.

"She said, 'No, I can't, I'm a woman.'" Kathy recalls her responding, and then: "The scales fell away from my eyes." She realized she could no longer ignore the sexism in the church. Kathy left and began shopping for churches again.

She came full circle, back to the Methodist Church. This one was larger and had youth groups. That was 2014. In July of that year, she went to her first Wild Goose Festival.

There, she had an epiphany. "I can be gay and Christian and here is what it looks like." Kathy remembered thinking. Before that, she had never known that she could be gay and Christian.

"Not that I was ever told it was wrong," she said. But that sentiment was in the air, and she had unknowingly internalized it. How many other Kathys out are there—talented, loving, funny, generous people — cast out of churches they want to belong to because of whom they love. And here is the most terrible thing about it. God is supposed to be about love.

A week after returning from the Wild Goose Festival, Kathy came out to her best friend. The friend was not shocked at all. Far from it.

"She said, 'Oh, that does make a lot of sense!'" Kathy remembered. That was how all but one or two people reacted.

Despite that positive response, it took her months to tell her parents.

"Were you scared to tell your parents?" I asked.

"Oh my gosh, yes!" Kathy replied.

She worked up the courage only after taking a four-day yoga instructor workshop that looked at the metaphysical side of yoga.

"It changed my life," she said, looking back.

She did not come out to her parents until March 2015, the result of three years of what Kathy described as arguing with God. Wild Goose presented her with the possibility that you can be gay and Christian. Yoga gave her permission to be who she is: a gay Christian woman.

Only then was she able to tell her parents. They were completely supportive of her. That was not surprising, she said, given that her parents had always been nothing but supportive of her for her entire life.

"It was much more me, what I had put on them, than what they had put on me."

Kathy was out, but her church didn't know.

"It's pretty easy to be in the closet when you're single," Kathy said.

She and Jes were now a couple, so she wanted to bring Jes into this important part of her life..

"I sat down with the head pastor. I said, 'I am gay. I need to bring my girlfriend. This is important.'"

"And he said, 'Yes, of course!'"

Kathy wanted some assurance that the couple would not have to worry about more conservative members criticizing them in a church that Kathy wanted to be a spiritual home for both of them. It's nuts and it's unfair that anyone should be concerned about the emotional safety of what should be a sanctuary for all. But the pastor reassured her. He knew his congregation. First, because Kathy was going to contemporary services, most of her fellow congregants would be more progressive. More conservative members would attend traditional services. And he felt that the nature of the congregation was such that if any member were to have any objections, they would come to him first.

Jes's re-entry to the religion took time. And, just as the Wild Goose Festival had helped Kathy, it helped Jes. In 2016, she went to the festival with Kathy.

The Goose is a hilarious place. It's in a stunningly beautiful setting, surrounded by the Blue Ridge Mountains. It's in a campground near where the Appalachian Trail and the French Broad River meet. In July, it is hot, humid and muddy. Small storm cells move in and out, pouring rain for a few minutes and sending everyone running for shelter. Then the skies clear.

It attracts New York Times best-selling authors, including Barbara Brown Taylor, for instance, the former Episcopalian minister, one of whose books is titled *Leaving Church: A Memoir of Faith*. As I mentioned earlier, I also listened to Nadia Bolz-Weber, Lutheran minister who ministers to outsiders. There was even a presidential candidate, Marianne Williamson (remember, she was among the twenty or so Democratic candidates in the early days of the 2020 race). And there are nationally known pastors devoted to social justice like the Reverend William Barber, co-chair of the Poor People's Campaign. He's behind Moral Mondays. This is a group that opposes what it calls immoral immigration laws, countering them with peaceful protests featuring hymns, prayers and marches at the border and at immigration centers.

On Easter Sunday 2017, he told his congregation in Goldsboro, N.C., that Jesus may have died for his sins, but the Romans hung him on the cross for sedition. Christ refused to bow to Caesar's oppression.

Barber continued "Caesar may be dead, but the spirit of Caesar is still alive," he says, "Because oppression still lives and hate still lives and racism still lives and meanness still lives and injustice still lives."[1]

That's the kind of preaching you hear from progressive Christians, those who marry social justice with their religion. And the Wild Goose Festival is where progressive Christians meet. The festival has been a place of epiphany for so many people who have been part of a Christianity with fences around it, fences that keep the other out. And that is a lot of people — the LGBTQ community, people of color (although the Goose needs more attendees of color, which it recognizes), refugees, immigrants and Democrats.

And so it was for Jes Miller, who confessed to being really nervous on the drive down, "We were really quiet, we listened to some audio books," she told me, remembering that trip from where the two lived in Virginia down to Hot Springs, N.C.

And after?

"I think I talked the entire six hours back," Jes said.

It was the summer of 2016, and one of the speakers was a woman named Jen Hatmaker.

Hatmaker was a wildly popular Christian author who is thoughtful and hilarious. I fell down laughing reading her blog post about doing Whole 30. I laugh whenever I remember her blog post about doing Whole 30. She describes it as a "Lazy Girl's Tale." I laughed throughout the entire column, but my favorite line was when her sister-in-law told her that the chorizo Jen had eaten had sugar in it.

Jen rationalized that it didn't count as cheating because she didn't know it and then she wrote that if she had wanted to cheat, it wouldn't be on a tiny bit of sugar in chorizo. "I would have gone face down in a trough of chips and queso with a wine chaser."

Now that is my kind of over-the-top humor and overall attitude about life. At the same time, even though she is now an adherent of Whole 30, she's an 80 percent adherent. That is, it's fine if there's a little bit of sugar in her ketchup and she can still put Almond Joy creamer in her coffee. That shows that she'll go over the top for a laugh, but when it comes to real life, she is a woman of reason. She is also a best-selling *New York Times* author and host of an HGTV show about how she and her former pastor husband renovated their house.

Hatmaker was long the darling of the religious right because she is so personable and relatable.

Until, that is, she came out in support of the LGBTQ community that spring of 2016.

Her Christian publishers pulled her books off the bookstore shelves and did the same with her husband's books, she said on the podcast, *Terrible, Thanks for Asking.*. One publisher said she could either pay to have the publisher ship the books still in its warehouse, "or we're gonna burn them." She took heat from all corners.[2]

"It was a really dark, and a really lonely, time," she told TTFA host Nora McInerny. And Hatmaker had *prepared* for the blowback. That's the nature of the religious right and its belief in a vengeful God. She knew she was going to pay a big price. A very, very big price.

But she had a clear choice, she told McInerny. She could have her career—which was a pretty damn nice one. Or. she could have her integrity. She could not have both.

"And so I picked my integrity, and I decided then I will stand in the storm. I will not reverse. I will not walk it back. I will not change my mind. I will not soften the blow. I'm just gonna take it."

Jes had never heard of Hatmaker but she went to hear her speak.

"She cried real tears and apologized for being part of a system that hurt us," Jes remembers. "That still brings tears to my eyes."

Jes remembers Hatmaker talking about how she regretting being part of a system whose decisions and viewpoints hurt people like Jes and Kathy. But that wasn't all that Jes found at the Goose. She loved being with other Christians who were comfortable worshiping outside the box, under a tent, in pouring rain, with everyone sweating in the relentless humidity.

"There is so much God and so much connecting with people," she says.

The Festival introduced her to a world that her sixteen-year-old self could not have imagined—a Christian world that welcomed, accepted and affirmed people like her and could fill her up with that kind of loving kindness that she could take back with her to her own community.

But her community, the United Methodist Church, was having a major battle over same sex marriage. In February 2019, delegates attending the General Conference of the United Methodist Church, a global organization, voted 438 to 384 to strengthen bans on LGBTQ practices.[3] This is a big deal—Methodists are the biggest mainstream Protestant denomination in the US.

Most U.S. delegates favored LGBTQ-friendly options. But conservative U.S. delegates sided with delegates from Africa and the Philippines and outvoted them.

The UMC probably will split over the issue. But the meeting to make the final decision was scheduled for May 2020. And, for obvious reasons, it has been rescheduled.

After the vote in 2019, at least three dozen members of the congregation told Jes and Kathy how upset they were with the decision.

Now that is affirmation on a local level.

Jes and Kathy had planned their wedding for April 2020. Despite the pandemic, they still got married, but guests attended virtually.

So one April day in 2020 I opened up Facebook and saw a beautiful and heartwarming scene. It was Jes and Kathy's wedding. They both looked beautiful, illuminated by an inner joy and love, not just between two people but two people uniting under the auspices of a loving God.

Even though it was virtual, the event was filled with love. That love manifested itself in online greetings from Jes and Kathy's friends and family and, most sweetly, perhaps, from Jes's mother, expressing her love for her daughter, Jes, and her new daughter Kathy.

In September, Jes and Kathy had a second wedding, one that more people could attend. My favorite photo (I think, there were a lot) of the two: their smiles are wide, and they are showing us the soles of their shoes, painted with rainbows.

Kathy and Jes's love story—with each other and with God—is emblematic of a massive change in the way Americans, secular and religious, view people through the prism of who they love.

In 2004, Americans opposed gay marriage, 61 percent to 31 percent. That has completely flip-flopped. Now, 61 percent of Americans support gay marriage and 31 percent oppose it.[4] What's more, that approval is true even when you look at the religious. Members of all major religious traditions in the U.S. are more likely than ever to support gay marriage.

Here are the mainline protestant churches that accept gay marriage: the Episcopal Church, the Evangelical Lutheran Church of America, the Presbyterian Church (USA), Quakers, the Unitarian Church and United Church of Christ.

Here is an important point. What issue is the one on which

the divide between Millennial evangelicals and their elders is greatest?

You got it: Gay rights.

Nearly twice as many millennial evangelicals, 43 percent, favor gay marriage than older evangelicals, at 23 percent.

When it comes to accepting homosexuality in society today, the numbers go even higher- *for both groups*. Fifty-one percent of millennials and 32 percent of older evangelicals believe homosexuality should be accepted by society.[5]

Look at Pete Buttigieg's 2020 campaign . Who could have imagined an openly gay *and* Christian man running for president even ten years ago?

The world is changing.

And may be why evangelicals and the right told bigger and bigger lies trying to frighten their flock into voting for Donald Trump.

Fear, sadly, is often a highly effective tactic.

But sometimes fear backfires. It's driving some evangelicals to turn their backs on fear mongering in the name of Jesus to find a new community with people of faith who preach love and social justice. It's prompting some to turn their backs on religion and God, period.

Let me introduce you to Kayla Cannon. Ex-evangelical.

---

[1] WOOTSON, Cleve W. "Rev. William Barber builds a moral movement. *The Washington Post.* June 29, 2017. https://www.washingtonpost.com/news/acts-of-faith/wp/2017/06/29/woe-unto-those-who-legislate-evil-rev-william-barber-builds-a-moral-movement/

[2] Jen Hatmaker interview, *Terrible, Thanks for Asking, May 26,*

2020. https://www.ttfa.org/story/2020/05/26/the-other-side-of-belonging-transcript

[3] " "Rift over gay rights comes as United Methodists in U.S. have become more accepting of homosexuality." February 26, 2019. https://www.pewresearch.org/fact-tank/2019/02/26/rift-over-gay-rights-comes-as-united-methodists-in-us-have-become-more-accepting-of-homosexuality/

[4] Attitudes on Same-Sex Marriage. Pew Research Center. May 14, 2019. https://www.pewforum.org/fact-sheet/changing-attitudes-on-gay-marriage/

[5] Diamant, Jeff. "Though still conservative, young evangelicals ae more liberal than their elders on some issues." Pew Research Center. May 4, 2017. https://www.pewresearch.org/fact-tank/2017/05/04/though-still-conservative-young-evangelicals-are-more-liberal-than-their-elders-on-some-issues/c

7

THE EVANGELICAL EXODUS

I met Kayla Cannon when she and I sat next to each other on a jet stuck on the tarmac at the Durango Airport in September 2019.

The day before, I had completed the Imogene Pass Run from Ouray, Colorado, to Telluride, Colorado. It's a 17.1-mile run over the 13,000-foot high Imogene Pass. For years, I had wanted to see if I could do it. And finally, I did. Out of about 1200 runners, I think I was finisher 1,190.

But I finished.

As I sat on that plane, I thought about all the other things I wanted to do that I had yet to try. One was to write this book. Lost in thought, I was slow to realize the young woman next to me wanted to chat.

Our flight to Phoenix, where I would get on a plane to New York and she would get on a flight to LA, was delayed.

So we talked.

I thought to myself as we exchanged our first tentative greetings, *What could someone from rural southwest Colorado have in common with me, a big-city liberal?*

A lot, it turns out. So much so that, secular as I say I am, a part of me still thinks God, did you, er, have a hand in this seat assignment?

Kayla was leaving her baby girl for the first time for a business trip. So she already was missing her adorable daughter (she showed me cute photos) but also excited to be her own person for a few days. I remember those days well and those conflicting feels of reluctantly leaving my kids but looking forward to being on my own.

More importantly, Kayla had been raised as an evangelical. And then rejected it.

Kayla grew up in Vermont and attended a private Christian school.

"In Bernie country?" I asked, surprised, referring to Vermont's Senator Bernie Sanders. She laughed and said it was unusual.

"It's not like the South," she said, "We were a weird pocket."

Her family attended a nondenominational Pentecostal church that taught a very literal interpretation of the Bible.

Kayla is smart, as in full ride to American University smart. She has an outgoing personality — as I could see by the way she opened up to me, a total stranger.

She talked freely about her horror when ICE conducted a raid and people she worked with at a restaurant in Telluride suddenly disappeared. Anyone with half an eye in any resort area knows how many workers are Hispanic and may be undocumented, or afraid of exposing a friend or relative who is undocumented.

I sat up in my seat.

"ICE conducted a raid in Telluride?" I was equally horror-struck. ICE is a constant in New York, packed as it is with people of color and immigrants. But in a remote mountain town like Telluride? Only 2,500 people live there. But it is a blue enclave. People in Cortez, which is seventy miles away and also blue, but surrounded by a lot of red, talk about the Telluride hippies — although in a town where the median home price is about a million dollars, you've got to be a pretty capitalist hippie.

ICE strikes tactically — resort towns and meatpacking towns as well as in big cities, which usually have far more diverse populations. It's all part of its strategy to terrorize and intimidate.

Kayla wasn't afraid to talk about that, or anything else, as it turned out.

Going to a secular high school and American University clearly opened her eyes to a much broader world than the one she'd been raised in. Early on, she had begun questioning the credos she'd been taught. She had an outgoing personality. She wanted to run for student council, but her conservative brethren talked her out of it.

Why? She was a woman. That kind of leadership position was for men. She was realizing that "I'm a strong woman who does not fit the biblical interpretation of what a woman should be."

She pushed her parents to let her go to Rutland Public High School in Vermont because the religious school she attended did not offer the advanced placement courses she wanted to take.

When she won her scholarship to American University, her parents were supportive. But, she said, they clearly worried about her move to a liberal school. Once she began attending American University, which is in Washington, D.C., she found herself intensely studying bills that were going before Congress.

"Being Republican was against everything I stood for and cared about," she realized.

One of her first friends at American University was flamboyantly gay. Her religion had taught her that it was her job to tell him that his lifestyle would land him in hell. She did not.

And then there were the gaping holes in the theology she'd been raised on.

"The Bible talks about divine intervention," she told me. But in a world where children starve and can be sold into the sex trade, she saw no divine intervention at all.

Growing up, expressing any kind of doubt was forbidden. To doubt was to sin.

She quit going to church while at college, although she continued to believe in God and still identified as a Christian. Then came the 2016 election and the swell of support among evangelical churches and their congregants for Trump.

"The way the Church championed Trump, that was when I could not associate with Christianity. Period. I was also angry at how many of my friends and family didn't talk to me for supporting Hillary," meaning Hillary Clinton in the 2016 presidential race.

Kayla lasted only two years at American University. She had long been plagued by anxiety and it peaked while she attended college. Her evangelical upbringing had taught her that everything, including things like anxiety and other emotional distress could be overcome by prayer. If she was suffering, it was because of her personal failure to fully embrace her faith.

She left American to stay with a cousin attending a conservative religious school, to try praying her mental health problems away. There she met her future husband, who was attending the school. His calmness and rationality helped her enormously. They fell in love and planned to marry. He went home to Telluride, Colorado, and she returned to her family in Vermont, where her anxiety spiked. And there, with her mother's support, despite evangelical doctrine, she finally got the professional help she needed.

She and her husband continued to wrestle with faith,

personally and as a couple. She sees this a lot among millennials, and some are leaving their churches.

"They are sick of having to hate because of their church," she said. And here is the problem for the religious right. Once these young people question one thing, the whole house of cards falls apart. Because, as Kayla sees it, conservative Christianity is based on absolutism and blind faith. So once there is room to question one thing, everything is open to debate.

Kayla stopped associating with any kind of religion and considers herself agnostic. She is not alone. Her best friend, whom she met at a Bible school she attended, has also renounced organized religion.

Twitter is a great way to find this community, she told me. Just use the hashtag #exvangelical.

That hashtag reminded me of Rebeca and Charlie Seitz and their podcast, *Freevangelic*.

These are two more people who told me the same thing. Once you ask one question, a torrent follows. I found Rebeca and Charlie on Instagram just before I went to Wild Goose. I had been using social media to connect with Wild Goose attendees, but we didn't manage to meet during the festival.

Having been reminded of the podcasters I missed at Wild Goose, I contacted Rebeca through Instagram. She is a blast, funny as hell. She can find the humor in terrible things. She told me how her parents became evangelicals. By age nineteen, her mother was married for the second time with two kids of her own plus stepchildren. It was a rough situation, Rebeca said. Neither of her parents were churchgoers, but Rebeca's mom found a conservative church that gave her a much-needed framework to help her handle her chaotic life.

Her mother does nothing halfway, Rebeca told me. She quit wearing shorts. Makeup was verboten. Rebeca compared it to someone going on a diet and throwing out everything in the pantry that has sugar or carbs. In her mom's case, it meant every book in the house was about religion and every song she sang was religious.

"My mom's finding faith was never going to be Lutheran," Rebeca said.

This embrace of a very conservative religion startled Rebeca's father. So he went down to the church to give that pastor a piece of his mind, or maybe even a punch in the face, according to the family story, Rebeca said. Instead, the pastor converted her father and baptized him.

It was such a drastic change that it alienated almost all of Rebeca's relatives. But it was the world into which Rebeca was born, and she knew nothing else. Rebeca grew up memorizing the Bible.

When she hit adolescence, her mother handed her a book by the right-wing guru James Dobson, *Everything You Need to Know About Adolescence*, and it was all about female subservience, Rebeca recalled. You can't call boys or ask boys out. You can't wear anything low cut. Your makeup has to look natural. There was an emphasis on your body because it was the temple of the Lord. But your sexuality was not about women, it was about how women related to men.

Rebeca matured physically early.

"I was very well-endowed from sixth grade on," she remembered. Ultimately, she had a breast reduction.

But throughout her childhood and adolescence, her family lectured her on her appearance. "Don't put on lipstick; don't look like a hussy."

A man sexually abused her when she was eleven.

"What were you wearing?" her mother asked when Rebeca went to her. And it happened again and again, in high school and in college. The response was always something to the tune of "you probably asked for it."

The worst was a summer she spent in Washington, D.C., working for a political spin-off of the ubiquitous James Dobson's Focus on the Family.

"My mom could not have been more proud," she remembered. "Her daughter would become a senator, pass these laws, then get married, have kids and home school them."

But the totally naïve Rebeca fell victim to a predator who slipped a date-rape drug into her Coke when she met him for pizza. She never knew exactly what happened that night.

Bewildered and frightened, she confided to a co-worker at her job at the right wing, religious think tank. Once again, she, not the abuser, was the problem. The think tank packed her up and sent her home to her parents. They refused to speak to her because she had shamed her family.

"In that world, there was not really an opportunity to deal with it. Because if something did happen, it was because you didn't manage your sexuality and keep it hidden," she said. Although her religion was traumatizing, it was the only world she knew. She embraced it. She studied it.

Like Kayla, she was taught that if you do not believe the Bible 100 percent, you are not a Christian.

After college she was married very briefly and then divorced. She decided to try dating. She was never going to get married again, but she could have a little fun, she thought to herself.

One of her co-workers suggested she try Match.com.

"I'm like, 'I'm sorry, I don't do that.' My friend is like, 'Well, it's either that or a bar!'"

Rebeca decided her friend had a point.

So she posted a profile on Match.com and went on a date. She described it as a thirty-eight minute date that was thirty-seven minutes too long.

"It was the worst date of my life," she said.

She complained to her friend. "Well, did he ask you out or did you ask him out?" the friend responded.

The man had asked her out. Asking a man was a whole new concept to Rebeca.

"He dared me to ask just one guy out on Match.com and then he would not nag me," she said.

So, when scrolling through options on Match.com, she came upon the opening line of Charlie's description of himself: "To understand me, you need to understand my faith in Christ."

She emailed and thanked him for his honesty. So many people hide their faith, she told him. In the exchanges that followed, he learned she had just bought a house that was a fixer-upper and offered to "rescue the damsel from the menacing paint bucket."

She broke all the rules about online dating and immediately invited him over.

Their second date was a Bible study date.

Her mother was leery. By that time, Rebeca's parents had liberalized a bit and become Southern Baptists. Rebeca's mom had never heard of Lutherans and asked Charlie if it was a cult.

"He said 'No, ma'am, we've been around longer than the Southern Baptists,'" Rebeca reported.

The Seitz family has been Lutheran since Martin Luther, Charlie told me. He's not exaggerating. "Martin Luther's personal physician was a Seitz."

Wow! I thought when I heard that.

"We have our own jokes," he said. His father was president of one congregation and his mother was the first woman to be vice president of that congregation. After Charlie left home, he was treasurer of the congregation he belonged to in Nashville.

"Then I met the beautiful, amazing woman I am married to," he said.

Being Lutheran was so important to Charlie that he told

Rebeca they'd have to be Lutheran. At the same time, he was willing to accommodate Rebeca. For example, infants aren't baptized in the Southern Baptist tradition. The Baptists have to be old enough to accept Jesus as their lord and savior and then be baptized; they always have a story about how they came to accept Jesus and got baptized. And Rebeca wanted Charlie to be able to tell their son about Charlie's own baptism.

The couple ended up in a part of Kentucky with no Lutheran churches. The choices were Methodist or Baptist, with the occasional Episcopal church. As a result, the family went to a Baptist church, the First Baptist Church of Fulton, Kentucky. Religion was the center of their lives. One example: The only nonreligious kids' books in the house were *Goodnight, Moon* and *Giraffes Can't Dance*.

Rebeca scanned everything that came into their home to make sure it aligned with their worldview. Their lives revolved around church. Rebeca started a women's ministry, and her company was a PR firm for Christian authors.

"Nothing was outside of the church," she said.

And finally, her rational brain had had it.

She'd read the Bible in its entirety every year, a not uncommon practice in the evangelical community

The Bible is not laid out in chronological order, but some Christians read it in chronological order. Rebeca did that. She began to notice contradictory passages right next to each other.

She was thirty-eight, and it had been a tough year. Her brother-in-law had brain cancer. Her sister and her mother-in-law had breast cancer. Charlie had been laid off. His father was dying of Parkinson's disease and her kids were having trouble in school.

"Everything was falling apart around us," she said. "I was already in a place where God and I were not friends."

As she sat at her kitchen table with her Bible, she hit the first of two passages that talk about King David taking a census in Israel and Judah. In one passage, in 2 Samuel, David does so at God's instruction. But in another passage, in 1 Chronicles, Satan tells David to take the census. In both cases, God then punishes David's people because David took the census.

Rebeca kept going over these contradictory sections. Had David and his people obeyed God or Satan? "When the repercussions for doing it [the census] are death, it matters who gave the directive," Rebeca told me in an email. She had tried to rationalize the discrepancy for years, but she could not do that anymore.

"Nobody did anything wrong and they're getting slaughtered," she said. David and his people had obeyed God. And the reward was death. "I literally closed the Bible and pushed it away from me," she added.

Once Rebeca stopped automatically accepting the Bible as written, she concluded that "this is not unconditional love! This is controlling, manipulative love! ... A God that you have to please and worship and mollify or he will be angry and smite you, that is not unconditional love. That is abusive," she said.

Like Kayla, once she questioned one thing, she began questioning everything. And that included the evangelicals' unwavering support of Donald Trump.

"If I don't want to support a misogynistic, horrible liar, that means I can't call myself an evangelical Christian because you have to check the boxes," she remembered thinking.

She did not tell Charlie immediately. He'd lost his job, his father was dying; the last thing he needed, she felt, was to deal with her loss of faith.

Charlie was having his own struggles with faith as he watched his father waste away and cancer ravage his mother and other family members.

"I asked myself, 'Where is God in all of this?'" Charlie told me. "My answer was, 'Hmm, be nice if he'd show up.'" He told Rebeca that "We need comfort and hope and kindness and grace."

It wasn't that Charlie expected sunny skies and roses all the time, but these were Job-level crises. And, by the way, Rebeca pointed out, Job loses his children and God gives him more, but that doesn't replace the kids he lost.

"Maybe there isn't this big guy in the sky who has got your back when the chips are down," she remembers thinking.

Charlie and Rebeca kept going to church with their kids, then ages ten and thirteen. But it got harder and harder.

Rebeca was the one who got the family up and out the door every Sunday. "Baptists are more hardcore than Lutherans," she explained to me. "And suddenly, I wasn't."

She quit saying bedtime prayers with the kids. She would tuck them in and have Charlie do prayers. They skipped church for a few weeks. They didn't miss it. But they did miss faith. They just knew the faith they had been pursuing was the wrong one.

She told Charlie, "I feel like I'm lying all the time. Whenever I talk on the phone with someone, they think I'm in lockstep with them." At lunch dates, someone would say, "Let us pray," and she'd think, "I suck at faking it."

So she announced her departure from her faith on Facebook and linked that to her post. Basically it said, "I'm out and here is why, it's the Bible."

The result was a firestorm of texts and phone calls asking why she and Charlie were leaving. Meanwhile, she and Charlie were trying to figure out if Christianity had a place for people who did not believe the Bible was literal.

Charlie's educational background had been in anthropology and archaeology, so he undertook a new examination of the

Bible from that point of view. He looked at church history and how the Bible came into existence.

"What I found is that the Jesus of the Bible and the Jesus who probably actually existed are two very different people." Charlie said. "That [real] Jesus was interesting, a firebrand radical and not this guy in long robes with a lamb at his sides and little kids around it."

That's exactly how I'd felt as a kid, looking at the Jesus on the cover of my catechism book.

Rebeca said there a lot are of people today doing what that Jesus was doing around 2,000 years ago. "We don't say they are Christ-like — but they are!"

Amen.

And Charlie added the historical context. For instance, some books were written for a Greek-speaking audience. He found that a virgin birth catered to Greeks, ensuring the Greeks would see God as, well, a god. Some were written with Jews in mind.

Their podcast, *Freevangelic,* became a way for them to share their research, thoughts and questions with other doubters. And they found an audience, listeners who told them, "I love your podcast but I can't tell anyone because I'll lose my job."

Rebeca understood that issue.

"Evangelicals are: You're either with us, or against us, there is no polite middle ground," she said in describing listener responses.

A couple of friends from Los Angeles contacted her. "We're so glad you're out of that cult," one told Rebeca. Her response: "I don't know if it's really a cult." And the friend said, "Trust me, honey, you'll figure it out."

Another friend in California, a female pastor — a no-no for conservative Christians — reached out to her. They had built their friendship on being women of faith. "Hey, friend," the pastor said to her, "there is a festival that might be the group you need. Ever heard of the Wild Goose Festival?"

She hadn't.

But off they went to the Wild Goose. The festival's affirmation of the LGBTQ community was at first a tough one for Charlie. He's a home brewer, so he worked in the beer tent. There he met Jacob, who was biologically female but identified as nonbinary, pansexual and polyamorous. Jacob preferred male pronouns. It was the first time Charlie had met and become friends with someone who was not binary. Their shared love of beer and brewing helped them bond. By the end of the weekend, Charlie had joined Sara Cunningham's Free Mom Hugs as part of the Free Dad Hugs team.

Their kids thought the trip was worth it, if only because their father could embrace people he once would have rejected. But Rebeca and Charlie were still asking: Is there a place in Christianity for people who don't accept the Bible as being 100 percent true?

They found their answer at a session called "Debunking Hell, the End Times, Inerrancy, Conversion Therapy and Other Fake Faith Claims: Why It Matters," run by Michael Camp.

Camp is a onetime conservative evangelical with the resume to prove it. During his twenty-five years in the evangelical movement, he was a missionary to Muslims and an aid worker to Africa. Then he had what he called a huge faith shift. He's published two books *Confessions of a Bible Thumper* and *Craft-Brewed Jesus*. The latter chronicles the discussions of disillusioned evangelicals and Catholics who met regularly — over craft beers — to study the early history of Christianity. Like Charlie, they found a narrative very different from what they had been taught.

In Camp's session, Rebeca popped the big question:

"Frankly, I am just here to find out if you can be Christian if you don't believe in the Bible."

Camp's answer: Yes. You can be.

"Oh," Rebeca remembered thinking, "that changes everything."

Both Rebeca and Kayla went through their own crucibles to come to a new understanding of themselves. Rebeca's stemmed from contradictions in literal interpretations of the Bible, but Kayla's was more about women's roles and gender identity.

Which leads us to that eternally fascinating topic.

Sex.

8
IF SEX IS SO BAD, WHY DID GOD MAKE IT SO FUN?

Growing up, us Catholic kids had a lot of metaphysical debates about sex and confession. And it was totally outside of religion class, where we did not talk about sex at all. We just absorbed the abstinence message out of the ether.

And ignored it.

The sex-is-a-no-no message originated with the one commandment that explicitly deals with sex, "Thou shalt not commit adultery." Narrowly defined, adultery is a married person having sex with a person he or she is not married to. But we knew what it really meant you couldn't have sex unless you were married. To the person you were having sex with.

Forget about that! A lot of us did not wait until we were married to have sex. Hence, all the massively pregnant brides in Monroe County and, in the old days, families whose youngest child was actually the oldest daughter's child.

Here is another of the realities of sex in my hometown: Of the half a dozen babies born in St. Mary's Hospital when my youngest brother was born, he was the only baby whose parents were married. I remember overhearing my dad telling someone that and how worried he was about those babies of young, single mothers.

This in a part of Wisconsin that for a while called itself God's Country.

Clearly, no matter what parents, nuns and priests said, a lot of us Catholic kids were going to fool around. But, we had to do some rationalizing because we had been raised on hell.

So what was sex? Was it only actual intercourse? Did blow jobs count? What about just plain old making out and having orgasms? Was there a difference if we had those make-out sessions in the choir loft or in a classmate's Rambler, which had a front seat that could lie down flat? The classmate was very generous about loaning it out. But did you want to confess what you did with your boyfriend with Father Frank Brickl, even in the supposed anonymity of the confessional?

We knew that if we had broken a commandment — or a corollary of it — we couldn't go to Holy Communion unless we first went to confession. You had to confess so your soul was pure enough for you to go to Holy Communion. And if you didn't go to Holy Communion, everyone knew you had done it with your boyfriend. But what if you didn't fully confess in confession and went to communion anyway? Would lightning strike? Or would God play a long game and wait until you weren't expecting it? It was a debate that was impossible to resolve. So after a certain point, we would just drink a lot of beer.

Such metaphysical debates were not limited to west central Wisconsin. They took place all over the nation. One of my cousins had a college friend from Texas. The friend's parents were very observant Catholics, and their daughter was one of the few students my cousin knew who even went to confession.

"So," my cousin asked her. "How do you handle sleeping with your boyfriend?"

"Oh that," said her friend in her strong Texas accent. "That falls under lying to my parents!"

Damn. I wish I'd thought of that!

If you didn't think hard enough, you risked believing that your choice was eternal damnation or the wrath of your mother. Or, worse, risking that Father Brickl or later, Father Bernard Kelly, might jump out of his seat in the confessional to see who was confessing. Or, having the priest you're confessing to say, very loudly, "You did what?"

I opted for the very narrow definition which says having sex means actual intercourse; that got me through high school and most of my freshman year at college. After that I went for an even narrower definition: no sleeping with anyone who was married or in a relationship with someone else. And I've stuck with that. Which I guess counts as a literal interpretation of the anti-adultery commandment.

Still, I've had moments of unease. Like when, at thirty, I was having a romp in the hay with my sexy boyfriend and my grandma had just died. Suddenly I wondered, *Can she see this?*

I was remembering one Friday night when I was in high school or college and it was my turn to stay at her house. Her kids had the questionable idea of having one of us grandkids stay overnight on weekends, rotating through our ranks. The idea was, we could help if she fell.

One weekend, it was my turn. That night, I went to a wedding reception at the Moonlight Pavilion, a Quonset hut turned party venue in a little town called Cataract that offered more opportunities for trouble and fun than any other spot in Monroe County. The Moonlight, which, sadly, recently closed, was pretty basic then, right down to six-holer outdoor toilets. No dividers. So there you'd be, sitting next to your old babysitter or your ex-boyfriend's mom.

I got back to my grandmother's about 4 a.m. tiptoeing up the stairs, bracing my hands on the walls of my grandma's staircase and avoiding the squeaky boards so as not to wake her. I was at the breakfast table at 7 a.m., ready for her fresh-squeezed orange juice.

"I heard you come in with the birds this morning, Kate," she said, pouring my orange juice.

Shit, I thought.

Grandma Rice was a formidable woman. We had horses off and on when I was growing up. When we were little kids, if we couldn't get a bridle on a recalcitrant pony, she'd step in. She'd march right into that dirt in her sensible, low-heeled shoes and floral print dress, handbag hanging off one arm and with her free hand, grab the horse by its mane.

"Here now," she'd say, sternly, to the now behaving pony.

And then, "Give me that bridle."

"Okay, Grandma, thanks," we'd say, embarrassed at the way we'd let that pony outmaneuver us, and hand her the bridle.

I eyed her warily across the breakfast table.

"Don't worry, Kate," she said, pouring milk on her Special K. "I've been to some pretty good parties at the Moonlight, too. I won't tell your father."

Vena Hemstock Rice was a party girl too!

She had six kids. So I thought that morning after her death as I lay in bed with my cute boyfriend, well, maybe she's just thinking, *I've had some fun in the sack myself. Don't worry, Kate.*

So, sex was something I enjoyed with only an occasional pang of guilt. Luckily, I never felt shame. However, I was terrified of getting pregnant, and all of my boyfriends were, too. Because one of my classmates got pregnant when we were in junior high (I was horrified that she got pregnant but so impressed that she had done it), I never had sex without birth control. (Side note: My classmate and her boyfriend got married when she was old enough, had more kids and were successful farmers. The last I saw her, she hadn't gotten fat either, debunking tons of myths about pre-marital sex forcing couples into miserable marriages and making you fat). I was lucky. I learned only recently that, for a lot of kids raised in ultra conservative Christian and evangelical homes, sex — even just kissing — outside of marriage was a definite soul-burner.

They lived in fear of their God-given sexuality.

This bit of my education began the night I arrived in Hot Springs for the Wild Goose Festival. I was with a crowd of other attendees sitting outside the Artisun Gallery and Cafe, which has excellent ice cream and a strong Wi-Fi signal. We sat outside the by-then-closed cafe, our faces lighted by the glow of our LED screens. That's when Nate Novero very politely asked me for the password for the Wi-Fi we were using.

He was at the festival, he said, because he was recovering from the purity movement, an extreme abstinence movement, powered by the religious right beginning in the 1990s. And when I say extreme, I mean, no dating and no kissing! I had been too busy in the early 90s with sex and parties, and later in the 90s with having babies (after I got married but just barely) to pay much attention to the purity movement, so Nate had to explain it to me. It had been huge, with massive rallies in stadiums all over the nation. Young people pledged to say no until they were married. They promised to not even think about sex! Fathers gave their daughters chastity rings. It had been a massive movement. Its legacy: millions of federal tax dollars still allocated every year to promote chastity.

Nate said his recovery was taking years. He was a docu-series producer and editor who had worked on films for Netflix, the Discovery Channel, the History Channel and National Geographic. He was also a former church camp pastor who had fully embraced the purity movement and had preached abstinence himself.

The woman he married had been raised Catholic.

"She was not in the purity culture. She was just a good Catholic girl," Nate said. Waiting was acceptable to her.

Their wedding night was exquisite, he said. Exhausted by their wedding day, they just slept together, naked, but no pressure.

"Magical," Nate said, "I'll remember it forever."

But the magic didn't last. Between their own childhood traumas and having been, to varying degrees, repressing their libidos instead of listening to them, they were unable have joyful sex and Nate told me their marriage became a sexless one. Ultimately, they divorced. Nate is working on recovery from the purity movement, not just for himself but for others. He's using his skills as a filmmaker and a podcaster to do that.

Of course, the concept of abstinence before marriage — especially for women — is nothing new. But this long-time principle scaled up in the 1990s with endeavors like the Southern Baptist Convention's "True Love Waits" campaign.[1] Nate and his wife were just two of thousands caught up in it. Rolled out in 1993, it included conferences, concerts and purity pledges, complete with those purity rings. Whatever interaction there was between a girl and a boy was supervised by her father.

Women are the purity movement's main target. Purity becomes a way to subjugate women, to quash sexuality and desire. The big message of all this, author Linda Kay Klein wrote in her memoir, *Pure*, is that women are stumbling blocks who can trip up innocent Christian men with their sexuality.

As I think about this, I am surprised at the rage boiling inside me. I have always hated the sexism inherent in religion, and it is not limited to Christianity. When I converted to Judaism, I took a ritual bath in the *mikveh*. Technically, the *mikveh* is supposed to take you from impurity to purity, but traditionally it's something observant Jewish women were required to do monthly, after their period. Men can use the *mikveh*, too, usually before celebrating shabbat or before holidays. It's supposed to be about spiritual purity, but if you do a little research, back in the day, women weren't supposed to have sex with their husbands after her period unless they'd gone to the *mikveh*. But that also made me feel that menstruating was dirty. Which it is *not!* Which is when she's probably most fertile. To my jaundiced eye, that was just another way of religion making sex about procreation, not pleasure, and making that uniquely female biological function, menstruating, dirty . The attendant at the *mikveh* I went to irritated me with continued questions about whether I was menstruating. I hated that because I felt she was telling me my period was dirty. Judaism's overall attitude about sex seems pretty positive to me — and looks really good now after learning about the purity movement. Still, I never did go back to that *mikveh*, or any other.

When I worked for a British magazine written for international business travelers, I did a story on the Middle Eastern country of Bahrain. When there, I took a tour of a mosque. Before I started on the tour, an older imam fussed over the burka I wore, telling me to push strands of my blond hair into the hood so you couldn't see my hair at all. He hated my sexuality. And I was in a business suit!

Meanwhile, a younger imam, who was the one who would lead my tour, stood grinning at me. That made the older imam angry. I told one of my work colleagues about it when I got back — the old imam who hated my Western womanliness and the younger man who was panting over it.

"That's because they think you're an American woman who sleeps with many men," my friend said, wickedly.

This view of woman as corrupter is as old as the story of Adam and Eve. The purity movement put that belief on steroids — and made it a moneymaking industry as well.

Nate had introduced me to one of the latest iterations of this view of woman as corrupter. And I learned a lot more when I sat in on a podcasting session he ran at the Wild Goose.

He was helping with a podcast called *Bible Bitches*. The "bitches" are two feminist, millennial ex-evangelicals who met at the Wake Forest divinity school. One is now a Baptist minister and therapist in Kentucky, the other an agnostic Californian. I had started listening to them before the Wild Goose. I highly recommend it. They pour bourbon into their glasses and do some biblical deep dives, augment them with facts and science (and a fair amount of profanity and jokes) to shine a progressive, feminist light on the many hypocrisies of the religious right.

In their podcasts, they talked about how the purity movement was not just about sexual abstinence. It preached shame. Sex — actual or in your head — that wasn't within the confines of a straight marriage was sin.

The movement targeted women, making virginity their most important virtue and constantly conveying the message that men were strong, women were weak — but woman had to take care not to tempt men with their female sexuality. How about that for shades of that cranky cleric at the mosque I visited in Bahrain?

The 1990s, when I did that mosque tour, was just when the purity movement was becoming a huge moneymaker that shamelessly hoovered up taxpayer dollars as it preached the joy of life untainted by sex. Purity purveyors like the Silver Ring Thing (which has changed its name) preached abstinence until marriage, and filled stadiums with kids who paid to attend and have their heads filled with purity propaganda. It had a panoply of young Christian rock stars giving these kids a soundtrack to not have sex to. Purity purveyors sold purity rings, albums, Bibles and more paraphernalia. And they didn't just sell stuff to their captive audience. They put out their hands to the federal government and received $1.4 million in federal funding.

The Silver Ring Thing hosted events starring kids who confessed to having been sexually active or admitted simply going on dates. On stage, they would bear witness to their sins and talk about how much better their lives had become once they turned their backs on sex.

There is a still a bit of the sixteen-year-old I once was inside me, and upon hearing that, she says, "You. Must. Be. Kidding."

Although an ACLU (American Civil Liberties Union) lawsuit ended federal funding for the Silver Ring Thing events, federal tax dollars still fund abstinence-until-marriage educational programs. Hundreds of millions of our tax dollars have funded such programs. That is despite solid research showing it is ineffective.

The problem with the purity movement is its overarching message, which says sex is bad and that kids who engage in sex or kissing or even thinking about sex are bad. Furthermore, women are both the temptresses and the enforcers.

The purity culture teaches that if a young man even thinks about sex, it's a sin. And women have to save men from sinning. In fact, if a man is thinking about sin, meaning sex, it's probably a woman's fault because she has dressed provocatively or worn makeup or said something suggestive or is just standing there breathing. The purity culture trains women to think about how they look to men. They are raised to look at what they want to wear and decide how a man will react to it. Anything a woman does has to take into consideration how a man will react to it.

Laura Barclay is one of the *Bible Bitches* podcasters. Raised in Kentucky, she was homeschooled using the fundamentalist ABeka and Bob Jones curriculum. Jones was the founder of Bob Jones University, a conservative Christian college that only opened its doors to Black students in the 1970s and only then because of pressure from the federal government. It prohibited interracial dating for the next thirty years. Only with the election of Barack Obama did it apologize for the racist policies of its past.

From home schooling Laura went to a Christian high school. Her parents were conservative, but not religiously conservative. They chose a Christian education for their daughter mostly because they were education advocates who didn't like their local school public school. They tolerated doubt and listened to Laura's questions.

"I was like, 'Ya know Mom, you tell me I can be president, but why aren't women preaching in the church?'" Laura remembers asking her mother.

"And Mom was like, 'I don't know. You stumped me.' And so we left church," Laura said, and then praised her mother for the move by saying, "I gotta give her mad props." When Laura interviewed at the Christian high school she ultimately attended, the implication of the interview was clear: no Philistines allowed.

"My mom and I just looked at each other during the interview process; my mom touched my hand, and there's non-verbal communication that passed between us and it was 'You just get the grades and the test scores and go to college, babe.'"

When Laura came home talking about a Bible class that taught students to recognize when demons were attacking them, her mother dismissed it as nonsense. That wasn't all the nonsense Laura heard.

"I had Bible teachers who were telling me Rome fell because of the gays," said Laura. "And the whole class erupted in laughter."

Sara Hof, the other half of the *Bible Bitches* duo, was also homeschooled with the ABeka and Bob Jones curriculum and attended a Christian high school. Her parents were far stricter than Laura's, discouraging any questions. So Sara had no one to counter what she learned in church and at school. She was totally immersed in purity culture, from home to school to church.

"It was a tangible commitment, a constant," she said.

She was taught that her body is a battleground between God and the devil; that Satan is constantly going after your soul. She saw that metaphor played out by an 80s group called the Power Team. These evangelical Christian bodybuilders toured the country performing feats of strength like ripping thick phone books in half and smashing concrete with their skulls in the name of God.

At one point during the show Sara saw, the lights went off, plunging the auditorium into darkness. When the lights came back on, the Power Builders told the audience, "We were fighting with demons in spiritual warfare."

"And now that sounds so silly, but we really believed it," said Sara. If you listen to the podcast, it's hard to believe a funny and irreverent woman like Sara bought into that one. But she did.

Both women were surrounded by the purity culture and were taught by their Christian educators to be ashamed of their sexuality. Laura gave one example of how her high school shamed its female students. Teachers hauled her and her female classmates into the chapel to measure their skirt lengths. They told those whose skirts the teachers considered too short how disappointed they were in them because sexuality was women's responsibility. The message: Men can't control themselves.

The week before a high school prom, Laura's school pressured students to sign a purity pledge. She refused.

"People were like, 'Are you going to sign it? Are you going to sign it?' I'm like, 'No, I'm not going to sign it.'" She was a virgin but believed her virginity, or lack of, was nobody's business. The pledge was counterproductive because of the administrators' narrow definition of sex.

"They only considered sex as hetero-normative penetrative sex. So these girls were signing it and just having anal sex," Laura remembered.

Crazily enough, Laura bumped into one of her male high school classmates when she was in college. He told her that her male classmates were placing bets on whether she was a virgin after she refused to sign.

"Well, were you?" he asked.

She refused to answer, just in case they were playing the long game and the bet was still on.

Laura is now a therapist. Helping people deal with religious trauma is part of her practice.

She explained to me that from a therapeutic perspective, our environment shapes a lot of our mental health. Repeated exposure to feeling shame about something — whether sex or something else — codes your brain. The more we hear a certain narrative, the more it imprints itself on our brains. When this happens in adolescence, as the brain is still developing, it cements these neural highways. Adolescents raised in conservative Christian traditions have shame over their bodies and their libido drummed into their heads no matter where they are: at home, at school and in church.

This neural mapping at such an impressionable age makes it far easier to trigger shame when these young people try to rewire their brains on their wedding nights. A married woman is supposed to have sex, but her brain has been wired in the opposite direction since adolescence or even earlier. You can rewire the brain, but it takes time to undo years of hearing that sex and the body are sinful.

Married couples who embraced purity in their youth have a hard time listening to a libido that they have repressed for so long. How can sex become fun for two people who have only viewed sex as wicked, as a symptom of their own sinfulness? Opening up is hard.

"If we're constantly told to feel shame about our bodies, we can't flip that switch," Laura told me. "If you're taught that the body is bad and dirty and something that will cause others to sin, then you can't feel comfortable or relaxed on your wedding night."

Which explains what happened to Nate and his marriage.

He and his wife divorced and are now friends. Nate has spent years rebuilding his life and trying to end sexual shame, not just for himself but for others like him. He took a hard look at himself, including how he had used pornography (the largest and most accessible source of sex education in the world, unfortunately).

He experimented with men, to see if he'd be struck by lightning.

"This is where God is supposed to show up," Nate said he remembered thinking as he recalled his encounter with a man.

"Did he?" I asked

"He did," Nate said. "In the form of grace and love."

With that, I had to pause the interview and absorb what he had just said.

We are all hard on ourselves — we're not good enough; we don't do enough; we don't do the right thing. And here was a moment when Nate jumped off a cliff, sexually speaking. And the world didn't end. Far from it. Instead, he found grace and love.

Nate is now in a heterosexual relationship.

He is an artist confronting his sexuality, with his camera as a tool.

"When I left my marriage, I left my faith," he said. "I didn't have anything to hold on to, and that scared the shit out of me."

He and his friend, Ryan Clark, an ordained Baptist minister, are working on a documentary about evangelicalism, what it has become, and how to deconstruct and reconstruct it.

As part of their work, they created a podcast: *The Touch, Conversations of the Spirit and Body*.

They recorded an episode of *The Touch* as well as one of the *Bible Bitches'* episodes at the Wild Goose Festival. I was right there, listening as hard as I could.

Nate and Ryan interviewed an icon of the purity movement for that podcast. She is Jennifer Knapp, the Grammy-nominated singer whose performances and music provided the soundtrack for the movement. You can hear their conversation in the October 11, 2019, episode of *The Touch*.

Jennifer performed in stadiums filled with thousands of people. Her breakout album *Kansas*, released in 1998, sold more than half a million copies. She won Dove awards from the Gospel Music Association of America for New Artist of the Year in 1999 and Rock Song of the Year in 2000. In 2001, her release *Lay It Down* was nominated for a Grammy. And then, in 2003, she walked away from it all. For years.

In 2009, she returned, with a new album and the revelation that she was gay.

Jennifer is bitingly funny. During the podcast she recorded with Nate and Ryan, she acknowledged the shame that gets laid on so many of us about sex and said that she has done a "shit-ton of shame shedding."

She has a master's degree in theological studies from Vanderbilt divinity school and, in 2012, she founded Inside Out Faith, a foundation that fights religious prejudice by working with faith communities to help them support LGBTQ inclusiveness.

At about the same time Nate and Ryan were recording their interview with Jennifer, another architect of the purity movement was renouncing it as well. He is Joshua Harris, author of the purity movement's bible, aptly titled, *I Kissed Dating Good-Bye*, and its follow-up, *Boy Meets Girl: Say Hello to Courtship*, and a third book, *Sex Isn't the Problem: Lust Is*.² He posted on Instagram that he had had a "massive shift in regard to my faith in Jesus." He also apologized for opposing same-sex marriage and LGBTQ rights.

Harris has called on churches to talk more openly about sexuality and asked his publisher to quit publishing the three books that were such a part of the purity culture.

He has also criticized evangelical support for Donald Trump, saying some of that support has been "incredibly damaging to the Gospel and the church."³

Bible Bitch Sara Hof has rejected the teachings she once embraced. She began having doubts about the world she had been raised in, which included the purity culture, toward the end of high school.

When I interviewed her in February 2021, she told me she had stuck to extreme abstinence until the summer after her senior year in high school, when she first kissed a guy. She attended a Christian college, where she found others who were testing the boundaries of their restrictive religious upbringing. She discovered that getting drunk did not instantly lead to addiction and began making out with guys, but without the benefit of any kind of model of a healthy sexual relationship.

That set her up for disaster.

She was fooling around with a boyfriend one afternoon in her dorm. And then, in a flash, the make-out session escalated fast, so fast that she was unable to recognize what was happening.

All of a sudden he was inside her.

What's he doing? she wondered. She protested and said "no," but not forcefully enough, she felt. She was doubtful — he had just performed oral sex on her. Even as she tried to stop him, she also felt she owed him.

"It was that trauma response where you just kind of do," she said, referring to the trauma response of appeasement.

She could not wrap her brain around the fact that she had just been raped. When she saw blood on her bedspread, she thought, *Oh! I just got my period*, and dug out a tampon.

"That's how disconnected I was," she said, looking back. It took her a solid year to even begin to deal with the rape. "My brain just couldn't process it," she said.

It was a classic situation. Purity culture — and, often, culture in general — teaches women to stay virgins but also teaches them to obey men. I hear women of all ages, women with grown children, women who are college students, talk about acquiescing to men. It doesn't necessarily mean sexual intercourse, it can be kissing or making out, but over and over, I hear women berating themselves for not standing up to men the way they feel they should and can. It's important for all of us to talk about it, so we don't feel as if we're some weakling betraying ourselves and our sex. We all have to recognize the forces of sexism that we are battling, in society, in the men in our lives and in our own heads.

Sara had a lot to wrestle with in college and grad school. As a philosophy major, she learned about existentialism. It rocked her world. Existentialism posits that people are free agents with control over their choices, and that societal restrictions inhibit free will and an individual's personal development. That took direct aim at the rules that had governed Sara's entire life.

It all left Sara angry, very angry at Christianity. Why? I asked her.

"The hypocrisy," she said. "You're supposed to love the other, unless they step outside of a very specific boundary." This conditional love did not make sense.

"If God is all powerful and good, why is there evil in the world?" she asked herself.

Sara went to divinity school to get a master's degree as part of the path to a PhD — but also to try to understand what religion meant to her and to understand Christianity.

Like her friend Sara, Laura was angry with Christianity — but not with God. She took a different route to divinity school. She was trying to help her sister, a recovering Southern Baptist, and her sister's husband-to-be, a recovering Pentecostal, find a place where they could get married. They had one condition. It had to be a venue that "wasn't angry."

The couple found a church like in Louisville, Kentucky. It was called Highland Baptist.

"I went and it was amazing and progressive and the sermons were about love and inclusion," Laura said. "I just remember making an appointment with the pastor and being like, 'Why don't other people do this?'"

That led to meeting Bill Leonard, then dean of the Wake Forest divinity school in North Carolina, who said that Calvinism is BS. Those are not exactly his words. Those are Laura's paraphrasing of his reaction to a theology based on strict moral codes and the belief that God runs everything, including your efforts to save your eternal soul. This, to Laura, was a revolutionary take on Christianity. And so, although she had never seen a woman in the pulpit, she went to divinity school.

Wake Forest was comfortable with Sara's and Laura's irreverence and doubt. Laura remembers learning that the Anglican Church was formed so England's King Henry VIII could divorce his wife and remarry. That was mind-boggling for her. Leonard taught his students to challenge every single assumption they held about religion. A lot of Laura's beliefs crumbled that first year at Wake Forest. It was frightening for her.

"I was afraid I was going to hell," she remembered. Although she had had many doubts about what she'd been taught at her Christian high school and college, she had internalized more of those teachings than she realized.

I've listened to a lot of the *Bible Bitches* podcasts. They challenge every precept far-right Christians teach. They do it with irreverence and wit. To learn that one of those women feared that what she was learning in divinity school might send her to hell is astonishing. It's a testament to her own courage in her search for truth. But it also shows the frightening power of a religion that uses fear to get its followers to toe the party line.

"My experience with my church and my world was very much 'guard against the world,'" Laura said. That world, she had been taught, would introduce her to beliefs that would send her to hell. And even as she picked apart those teachings using her rational mind, her gut was still afraid.

"Fear is a huge part of the fundamentalist strategy," she said. It's a control mechanism.

When Leonard told her class that the Song of Solomon was all about sex, it made Laura so uncomfortable that all she could do was laugh. "I never got proper sex ed training," she said. Laughter was a coping mechanism.

When Leonard said that doves meant breasts and nard meant lubricant, she kept on laughing.

Wake Forest introduced Sara to feminism. After she earned her master's of divinity at Wake Forest, she went on to earn another master's, this one in applied women's studies at Claremont Graduate University in California. Laura went on to earn a master's in marriage and family therapy and counseling at Louisville Presbyterian Theological Seminary. And, although Sara is now agnostic and Laura, besides being a therapist, has worked as a minister at Highland Baptist, they can still finish each other's sentences when it comes to skewering evangelicalism and how it hurts society.

Evangelicalism's insistence that women are weak and men are strong helps fuel domestic violence at a time when conservative churches practice biblical counseling. Pastors advise women to follow church beliefs that a loving and obedient wife is submissive to her husband.

"One woman said her pastor told her to pray more and submit more, like this is somehow going to make it better. It doesn't, actually, it just keeps fueling the problem," said Laura at one point during the podcast recorded at the Wild Goose Festival.

The result, she said: "More violence tickets are handed down to the next generation."

"I feel like 'pray more, submit more' is just code for 'you frigid bitch,'" Sara said.

I am with her on that because I heard the same thing although I was married to a liberal New York Jew, not an evangelical. Misogyny is not limited to conservative Christianity. Not at all. It is institutionalized in our society.

My ex-husband told me he was only a tenth of the man he could have been — and that was my fault. (He did apologize later, saying that he didn't remember saying that and if he had, he should not have.) One of the many reasons he told me he had decided to end the marriage was our sex life. And the problem was me and what I did not do or did not do enough of. There was truth in some of it. Because I can only deliver to lovers who are mostly kind to me. Also, it would have helped if he would have said. "I like this, can we do more? Or can we see if you like this?"

Obviously, as the first of the five marriage therapists we went to told us, we had major communication problems.

And our communication problems hurt our sex life. Sex is part of the whole package of a relationship. We had each brought our own unrecognized misogynist imprints into our marriage. And just emotional baggage in general.

I considered myself a feminist. That was my smarty-pants prefrontal cortex. Once I became a mother, that wily subconscious of mine fired up, and I believed that, as had my own mother, I was responsible for running the home front. My mother was a stay-at-home mom who managed home and family with almost total autonomy while my dad brought home the bacon.

My mother went back to work once the last of her five kids was in high school. In contrast, I was always a working mom, usually with one full-time job and some freelance writing on the side. But, like my mother, I also did the bulk of the traditional women's work, including childcare. My husband prided himself on being a new age man, but he usually only cooked when others were around to see — and told me what I was doing wrong with our kids. I did most of the after-school programming, shuttling kids myself (which I loved to do) or arranging for caregivers to do it. When I left town on a work trip, I left frozen meals in the freezer and lengthy scheduling notes.

Until the rise of the internet and user-generated content (which is free, unlike freelancers) blew up my freelance model, I was the rainmaker for the freelance work we both did that gave us the extra money we needed that helped us buy the first two of the three apartments that we combined into one.

I look back on those days and remember a jingle for an Enjoli perfume commercial I heard a lot in the 1980s. It painted the picture of the woman I thought I could be, a woman who could "bring home the bacon, fry it up in a pan and never let you forget you're a man."

But like the purity movement, that commercial — supposedly an anthem for women's liberation — charged the woman with responsibility for making her husband feel like a man. While keeping her in the kitchen.

And I swallowed it. Hook, line and sinker.

To be clear, it wasn't just institutionalized sexism that wrecked our marriage. I went for a guy who scared a lot of people, thinking our love could overcome all. I can hear Linda Ronstadt singing the lyrics to *Desperado* and remember how I thought that was us.

My husband could be funny as hell. I though he was cool. He was a rock climber and a great guy for hiking and camping. He was a skier who loved traveling fast down long, groomed runs. I went for the moguls, the steep fields of bumps, although they scared me. Probably because they scared me. And he'd do the moguls with me, saying good-naturedly, "The things I do to stay married."

I still miss that guy.

But he also had a cruel tongue. People just stopped showing up at our house. One friend told another that my husband was the reason he had quit coming to our parties. "He's too big of an asshole," the friend said.

Early in our relationship, we hired two sisters to clean our apartment. They worked for a neighbor who praised their work, so we hired them. I loved the way the apartment felt every time they came. It was clean and orderly and emanated calm. I told them that. But my then-boyfriend didn't like what they did. He told them so. I don't know what he said to them. All I know is that one day they finished cleaning, and then very politely gave me the keys to our apartment.

"We can't work here anymore," one said as her sister looked on solemnly.

I don't miss that guy, not at all. At the time, though, I stuck with my man.

In college, I had tended bar at the NCO Club at Fort McCoy,

an Army base near my hometown. There were a lot of Vietnam vets, and their anthem was Tammy Wynette's hit, *Stand By Your Man*. I think I heard it a few too many times. My husband would lose his temper or make me feel badly about something I had done or not done. I'd be upset, but Tammy would explain it all to me.

I've learned a lot since we split and I'm still learning. One thing I've learned was that my ex thought that a lot of what he did was okay. And it's because our society taught him that behavior — or much of it — was okay behavior for a man. He's not the only guy I've encountered like that. When I tentatively dipped my toes into the online dating scene, I met another guy who thought it was okay to criticize me, call me heartless and hope that I'd fall for someone who would break my heart. (Er, I have checked that box already!) And all this after exactly two dates — during which he hadn't paid for a single thing!

It was discomfiting, but it was also enlightening. Not only did these men think talking to me like that — as if I were a punching bag — was okay. I thought somehow I was responsible for their actions. Such experiences showed me how centuries-old norms still drive our lives, how despite our firm beliefs in independence for women, we have a long way to go. It's hard to shake the models we watched as we grew up.

"You think you're married to the same man Mom married," one of my brothers told me. I hate it when my younger siblings see things so much more clearly than I do! He was right, of course. My mother had put my dad on a pedestal (although she wasn't afraid to tease him, and he loved that). I modeled that behavior in my marriage. I internalized and lived it without even realizing it. Major score for that ol' subconscious!

Sexism and misogyny live not just in religion but throughout our culture and in our personal lives. Sexism in one sector reinforces it in the others, nurtures it and intensifies it across every facet of our lives. But, we can fight it. The *Bible Bitches* podcasters recommend the Unitarian Universalist Association's Our Whole Lives: Lifespan Sexuality Education, describing it as one of the best educational packages out there.

Our Whole Lives, or OWL, describes itself as providing honest and accurate information about sexuality. It's designed to dismantle stereotypes; it aims to build self-acceptance and self-esteem, foster healthy relationships and improve decision-making. OWL has half a dozen different curricula designed for varying age groups and periods of our lives. They are developmentally appropriate. It has separate curricula for kindergarteners and first graders, elementary school, middle school and upper school. These programs include parents. There are also curricula for young adults, adults in their middle years and older adults.

The *Bible Bitches* podcasters also recommended going to Planned Parenthood for programming, for use in churches, communities or schools.

There are other resources for those recovering from the purity culture. One of those places surprised me: the Alliance of Baptists on the Vanderbilt Divinity School campus (right, where Jennifer Knapp, gay rock star, got her master's degree).

This Baptist organization was an incubator for Nate and Ryan's just-released film: *Purity: Evangelicals' Legacy of Shame.* This yearlong series (go to www.puritymovie.org) grew out of a JUST SEX conference the Alliance of Baptists sponsored. It's a place where Baptists (yes, Baptists) tackle sexuality head on with some of the leading minds of progressive Christianity. These are people like the Rev. Bromleigh McCleneghan, author of *Good Christian Sex: Why Chastity Isn't the Only Option — and Other Things the Bible Says About Sex,* and the Rev. William R. Stayton, Baptist minister, psychologist and adjunct associate professor at the Graduate School of Education at the University of Pennsylvania. These speakers and others had been using Nate and Ryan's *The Touch* podcast as a resource for dissertations and essays. There are so many progressive Christian resources out there! It's all about shining a spotlight on them and then working with them.

This is where it gets political. When they recorded their podcast at the 2019 Wild Goose Festival, the Bible Bitches told their audience to hold their representatives in Congress accountable.

"Fuel that rage into action, y'all," said one of them. "It's the only way we can change anything."

And sometimes, churches can be part of that change. You can find those churches in unexpected places.

Amen.

---

[1] INGERSOLL, Julie. "How the 'extreme abstinence' of the purity movement created a sense of shame in evangelical women." *The Conversation*. December 10, 2019. https://theconversation.com/how-the-extreme-abstinence-of-the-purity-movement-created-a-sense-of-shame-in-evangelical-women-127589'

[2] Klett, Leah MarieAnn. "Joshua Harris marches in pride parade after apologizing to LGBT community." *The Christian Post*. August 5, 2019. https://www.christianpost.com/news/joshua-harris-marches-in-pride-parade-after-apologizing-to-lgbt-community.html

[3] Folley, Aris. "Ex-evangelical pastor says supporting Trump has been 'damaging' to church." *Politico*. November 4, 2019. https://thehill.com/blogs/blog-briefing-room/news/468844-ex-evangelical-pastor-joshua-harris-says-supporting-trump-has-been-damaging

9

MONTEZUMA COUNTY: PARADOX AND PARABLE

Montezuma County in southwest Colorado is beautiful and brutal.

It's in the Four Corners, where Colorado, Utah, New Mexico and Arizona meet. Montezuma County holds a lot of lessons for those of us who love our country and are fighting for its future. The place reinforces some stereotypes about the red and rural West. But, it challenges them at the same time. It looks solid red on political maps, but it is really purple. Reddish purple, but still purple. There are progressives here. Although, in the words of one, "It's a scary place to be a Democrat."

I spend a lot of time in Montezuma County, visiting my brother, Tom Rice, and my sister-in-law, Kelly McAndrews. I've been taking my kids there since they were small. They were born in delivery rooms on Fifth Avenue, worlds away from the rural America where I'd grown up. I loved that I could see Central Park from my hospital bed. But, and this is a big but, I wanted to make sure they grew up knowing what their country was like west of the Hudson River. Montezuma County was a perfect place for them to learn just that.

When my older daughter was five months old, I took her to

two family weddings. The first was my cousin's wedding at the Cosmopolitan Club, a 110-year-old private club for women with staircases with gilded bannisters, crystal chandeliers and garden terraces. It's set on pretty block on New York's Upper East Side and its distinguished members have included Eleanor Roosevelt, Marian Anderson and my Aunt Liz, who belonged to it for decades.

The second was Tom and Kelly's wedding in Montezuma County. It was in their backyard, with horses in the paddock and hay bales for an altar. I didn't just visit Montezuma County for my kids. I went there for myself, because I love Tom and Kelly and their kids, because I love the mountains and because, as years went by, it was a place with soul, a place whose beauty could help me heal my lacerated heart.

On my daily runs in Montezuma County, I am on high plains surrounded by four mountain ranges — the San Juans, the Abajos and the La Platas and the Utes. One peak is considered sacred; known as the Sleeping Ute, it looks like a sleeping warrior. Faith, a lot of different faiths, are woven into the fabric of Montezuma County. This is an icon of one of the first ones. I always see it when I run. When I visit Montezuma County, I try to stay in a place with views of the Sleeping Ute. Often, that's a trailer on Tom and Kelly's property.

During the summer monsoon season (yes, Colorado has a monsoon season!), clouds pile up and unleash some fearsome lightning storms. On a couple of summer visits, my kids and I stayed at an Airbnb with a rooftop deck. From there, we watched the clouds stack up, darken and then shoot lightning forks earthward. These sky shows are stupendous. And destructive, too, starting forest fires that pile smoke high in the sky. Many's the time I've watched those clouds of smoke, or looked down from a flight out of Durango at the forest fires below.

These fires can burn for days. An eight-day fire in June 2021 burned not just trees, pasture, plants and buildings but more than $6 million in taxpayer dollars.

We taxpayers spend millions — per fire — fighting those blazes paying for firefighter crews, trucks, planes, helicopters and fire retardant. Firefighters on fire engine crews carry chainsaws, fire shelters, water and piss packs. Piss packs are bags of water with hand pumps. The firefighters are wearing fire retardant pants and jackets and helmets. It is damn hot work before they even get to the fire. Then there are hotshot teams whose members travel light. These are usually twenty-person crews and they carry hand tools and chainsaws. They are famous for working long, strenuous days in steep terrain where engine crews don't go. They're the elite.

Even when it does rain, the puddles dry in less than an hour. And it's just getting dryer and dryer. Montezuma County is in the 21st[t] year of a drought.

"Just like back in ancestral Puebloan times," one old-timer told me.

The ancestral Puebloans, who lived here from about 600 to 1300 CE, created what became Mesa Verde National Park, one of the gems of Montezuma County. Fifty thousand acres of mesas, with natural alcoves that made this area the perfect place for the ancestral Puebloan cliff dwellers. They carved homes out of rocks. These could house a few families or be far more ambitious; they also built multistory grand palaces that could hold hundreds. In the land surrounding Mesa Verde, they built networks of lookout towers, roads and towns.

The ancestral Puebloans' story — and their mystery — grabbed me when I first learned about them in the 1980s. You see their petroglyphs on cliffs while hiking or river rafting. They even show what appeared to be *mammoths!* Theirs was a robust civilization that extended hundreds of miles. They cleared roads to connect communities and read the skies to determine when to plant and harvest crops. They were potters and basket weavers. Their trade routes stretched as far as Mexico. Some of those traveling traders probably stayed, according to Fred Blackburn, an American historian, educator and author who is the fourth generation of his family to live in this beautiful, arid land. He believes there were wave after wave of migrants to Montezuma County over the centuries and, when hard times hit, as they inevitably do, they fought.

These ancestral Puebloans thrived for centuries before they mysteriously vanished. Archaeologists have their theories: A twenty-plus-year drought hit, followed by 150 years of sparse and unpredictable rainfall. Then, perhaps because of the strain the drought put on food systems, violence erupted, possibly as a tool of social control.

My sister-in-law Kelly is a cowgirl. She can load two horses on a trailer more easily than most women load groceries into the back of an SUV. She actually does cattle drives. She also is an archaeologist who has covered most of Montezuma County and other parts of the Four Corners in every way a person can: on horseback, on foot, in four-wheel drives, on skis, occasionally on a mountain bike and, most impressive of all, on a helicopter flying through the winding canyons in which these ancients lived, worked and died.

One summer night as we watched the sun set behind the peach trees in her backyard, with the Sleeping Ute behind them, she told me a story over cocktails. In the 1990s, she was a leggy young archaeologist who would tie back her long blond hair on hot days spent working a promising site.

At one particular site, modern plows had disturbed the surface of the ruin, but as in often the case, once she got beneath the plow line, a treasure trove began to emerge.

It was an exciting site because the midden, where families who lived there would throw their trash, was unusually dense. It showed that people had lived at the site for a very long time. It was a complex of buildings constructed in a way that protected occupants from cold winter winds and the hot southwestern summer sun. When Kelly's group started working on the site, Kelly thought they might even find a tower. These are relatively rare finds.

There wasn't a tower but it was still a good site, one with masonry walls of beautiful stacked stone; at many points, Kelly and her crew could still see the plaster and paint on the walls. These were sophisticated builders.

The site was full of artifacts and during that summer, it was a happy place to work. Kelly and her crew arrived every morning, carefully pulling the plastic covers off the structures, admiring the beauty of the stone as they continued uncovering the lives of those who had lived there so long ago.

Autumn arrived. The days were still warm, but the mornings and late afternoons started to get chilly in the high desert.

"We were digging down and we were not yet to the floor of the kiva," Kelly remembered. The kiva is a subterranean part of the house, about six feet deep and roofed over, with the roof being the courtyard of the house above. Kivas are used for both ceremonial and everyday purposes, so it's an important part of the house and an exciting stage of excavations.

That's when the archaeologists found something they had not seen at this site before.

A broken human bone.

As they worked, they found more. They were everywhere. Not a single human bone had been left whole. Skulls were fractured, and even the tiniest of bones had been snapped. Bones had been crushed and scattered through the rooms. Some had been burned and left in the hearth. The dig took on a different tone and the chill Kelly felt was not just from the air.

Now, when they gently pulled off the tarp, they weren't looking down at a thing of beauty.

They were looking down at the scene of a mass murder.

The hair on the back of my neck stood up when Kelly first told me the story and it still sends chills down my spine.

They began cataloging the bones, in order to determine how many victims there were and who they might have been. It appeared to be an entire family. Little kids. Older people. It was destruction with terrible intent. It was horrifying. That evening, Montezuma County showed a different part of itself to me.

Kelly is a scientist, so she and her colleagues looked beyond the horror for the reason. Why did the killers have to so completely destroy this family?

Here was the really scary part. This was not a single incident. It was part of a pattern. This kind of murderous mayhem had happened at at least seven other sites in the area. It was part of a larger cultural event, but archaeologists and historians can only speculate about the cause. They have been able to determine that, before they were massacred, the people who lived at the site Kelly and her team excavated had persevered through twenty years with little water. The drought had worsened by about 1150, when those in Kelly's site and the other seven settlements were wiped out.

There are many theories.

One theory: intimidation. Perhaps one group blamed the endless drought on another group. They could have considered them witches and killed them to eliminate those they blamed for the drought. Or, the killers may have used violence to frighten people into obedience or to eliminate nonconformist behavior. This theory posits violence as social control.

These ancients drifted away, migrating to other parts of the Southwest, leaving behind their architecture, pottery, roads and a mystery.

Montezuma County has seen wave after wave of immigrants ever since. There were the Indigenous peoples: Apache, Navajo and Ute. Then came the colonizers: Spanish conquistadors and then Americans pursuing their "manifest destiny" of expanding the nation's borders from the Atlantic to the Pacific. There were Civil War veterans from both sides, miners, cattlemen and farmers. And they all brought their religions: Catholics, Methodists, Mormons and Seventh Day Adventists.

The relationship between those who arrived earlier and those who arrived later is always the same. Cautious circling, uncertain detente, fear and suspicion, cooperation — especially against a common enemy — and sometimes, love. Or lust, at least. Sometimes, they worked together. Sometimes they married each other. Sometimes, they fought each other. And sometimes, they killed each other.

It all combined into a combustible pile of conflicting property claims and layers of prejudices that created in which earlier arrivals felt they outranked those who came later, Blackburn told me when I interviewed him about the county's history.

Mormons worried about the non-Mormons, Mexicans worried about the Anglos, veterans looked down on Native Americans. A Ku Klux Klan chapter formed in a Methodist church in Durango in the late 1800s or early 1900s; it was really more of an anti-Catholic move than anything else, Blackburn told me in one of our interviews.

And it was all happening in an arid land, where everyone fought for water, a place where settlers attracted by 160-acre parcels of land the US.government gave to settlers under a series of homesteading acts. All these groups had to struggle to survive, just as the ancestral Puebloans had.

Place names tell the story of how harsh a land it was. El Rio de Nuestra de Señora de Dolores (the River of Our Lady of

Sorrows) was shortened to the Dolores. It goes through the small town of Dolores.

And then there's Disappointment Valley, which stretches through San Miguel and Dolores counties, which are right next to Montezuma County. Early explorers thought they'd found a creek, but the creek ran dry. Hence, they named it Disappointment Creek, and the valley it sometimes flowed through got its name.

In the 1800s and early 1900s, Disappointment Valley was as fine an example of the Wild West that you could find anywhere. Once, a mob broke into a jail to lynch suspected thieves, not bothering with a trial. Then, a posse of cowboys galloped up to the jail. They reined their horses to a halt, then casually pulled back their jackets to reveal their guns. The crowd drifted away; the accused thieves survived.

A local cowboy led a gang that robbed the San Miguel Bank in Telluride, Colorado. The robbers escaped by riding hard through Disappointment Valley, where someone, no one ever really knew who, but there was a lot of winking going on, gave the gang fresh horses. That cowboy-cum-gang leader later took the name Butch Cassidy, partnering with a cowboy calling himself the Sundance Kid.

Every once in a while, vestiges of that Old West pop up in Montezuma County. I've been in a car caught behind cowboys moving cattle, plodding peacefully down Highway 145 just outside the town of Dolores, as they're herded from high summer pasture down to lower pastures for winter grazing. I, of course, love these scenes of the Wild West, a land without fences and gates to close. And Montezuma County is still home to lots of cowboys, cowgirls and their horses.

But you're more likely to see trucks on highways than cowboys on horseback. A lot of them are big trucks, trucks used for ranching, farming, construction work and mining.

They're the workhorses for people in Montezuma County today.

There are the ever-popular Ford 150s, big Ram trucks and Toyota Tacomas. Tacomas are a solid truck. Ram trucks are big powerful trucks named for an animal so combative that its name is also a verb. Rams often settle disputes by slamming their heads together. Knowing that, you might have expected any Tacoma Toyota truck would sport a Biden-Harris sticker (if it had one at all) and any Ram truck would be flying a giant Trump flag and possibly a Confederate flag as well.

Sometimes that stereotype is correct, but not always. In Montezuma County, surprises await.

Years ago, I met one of those surprises at my brother Tom's kitchen table. Monty Risenhoover is six foot three and weighs a lean 190 pounds. Even next to my six-foot-tall brother, he looks big. Laugh lines are carved into his face, sun crinkles sit around his eyes. Monty, his eyes twinkling, once told me I looked like Tom's younger sister. I was twelve when Tom was born. I'm a Monty fan, of course.

Monty has three trucks. Two of them are Ram trucks. One is a 2013 4WD that Monty uses for what he calls cowboying. It's always hooked up to his trailer. It's the one he uses when he goes riding with my cowgirl sister-in-law. Another is his mining and oilfields truck, a 2019 Ram truck, a four-door with an extended cab. And then there is his old Ford truck, which he uses for hauling hay.

Monty is the third generation of his family to live in Montezuma County. His father gave him his first bucking horse at age seven, and he's been cowboying ever since. Like his father and grandfather before him, he's made his living breaking horses, working oilfields and running trading posts. He's been a cowpuncher in Wyoming, poured concrete in Texas and dug mine shafts in Colorado. He's lived out of his Jeep more than once. And once, he told me, he lived in my brother's trailer fifty miles away in Bluff, Utah.

The Risenhoover saga is an American epic, a constant quest over generations for a place to call home that lets you make the kind of living that can feed and house a family. It can be hard to do that in Montezuma County — and in a lot of other parts of America as well.

Monty's a hell-raising cowboy and miner and the son of a hell-raising cowboy and miner. He admits to smoking a little weed now and then, but no longer drinks the way he used to "except for a little red wine and tequila."

He takes pride in being a registered independent — you really can't expect a guy like Monty to ever let anything except maybe a woman claim him. And even then, he seems like the kind of guy who responds best to a light hand on the reins.

With friends from across the political spectrum, he's usually low key about expressing political views, taking his grandparents' advice to avoid talking religion or politics. "Unless," he says, "I get drunk and rant." Q

Monty, however, is a political realist.

"Democrats don't stand a chance in Montezuma County," he says.

That said, he's voted in every election since he was eighteen. He always voted for Ralph Nader because he was the green candidate.

About the presidents:

He described Ronald Reagan as "a piece of shit," but had kindlier feelings about George H.W. Bush.

He thought Bill Clinton "was pretty good man, and much like all men, had his faults. And I can sympathize with a guy who likes women."

George W. Bush?

"I couldn't stand that guy," he said, mainly because he started the Iraq war.

He described himself as "all behind" Barack Obama because of his eloquence and all-round decency. He voted for Hillary Clinton — although that was more of an anti-Trump vote because Monty has nothing but disdain for Donald Trump.

And everyone he knows knows it. So of course, he voted for Joe Biden, as well. I've introduced you to Monty Risenhoover because he's the kind of guy we all need to know, partly because he is a good story and he's a great storyteller. He's exactly the kind of independent rogue right-wingers would want to claim as their own. But they can't. Because he won't let them. Monty Risenhoover is why we need to look beyond maps that break counties, states and the nation into maps of red and blue and recognize that this a nation of red, blue and purple. There's nuance out there and we Democrats and moderates have to pay attention, especially in rural America, now more than ever.

The people of Montezuma County are white, Ute and Navajo, Hispanic, Republican and Democrat. There are a lot of lawns with Trump signs and trucks flying Trump banners and Confederate flags — a reflection not just of the white nationalism of a racist right romanticizing a total and humiliating defeat but the heritage of those Civil War veterans who showed up from the South a century and a half ago.

And then there are signs that bespeak a different philosophy. They're another reason that I say Montezuma County is really a purplish red. You know these signs; they say:

W*E* B*ELIEVE*
Black Lives Matter
Women's Rights Are Human Rights
No Human Is Illegal

Science Is Real
Love is Love
Kindness Is Everything

Or

Humankind
Be Both

THE POPULATION of Montezuma County has only about 26,000 residents; around 8,700 of them live in Cortez, the county seat.

According to the website Best Places, of the campaign contributions made in Cortez, from 2015 to 2018, 2,307 donors gave $70,555 to the Democratic Party and liberal campaigns, averaging $31 per contribution. In contrast, there were 245 contributions totaling $51,461 to the Republican Party and conservative campaigns. Average contribution on this front? $210.[1]

In the 2020 election, 40 percent of Montezuma County voters chose Joe Biden, up from 33 percent who voted for Hillary Clinton in 2016.

There are islands of progressive activism. I wouldn't call them challengers to all of those right-wing flags. I would call them leaders of their own movement.

I saw a few of these leaders in the street over Labor Day weekend in 2020 when I was back in Cortez. I was running errands in town one Saturday morning and saw a march, 70 to 100 people carrying Black Lives Matter signs, handmade signs proclaiming the rights of Indigenous people and signs about respect, peace and unity.

Marchers included little kids holding their parents' hands, teenagers and twenty-somethings, middle-aged and older. They walked on the sidewalk, talking to each other, crossing the street on the crosswalk, completely within the bounds of the law and common civility.

When I saw the march, I stopped. I watched. I cheered. My heart soared. Cortez was the last place I expected anything like this to happen. It was so heartening.

I heard the trucks before I saw them. Drivers revved their engines and lay on their horns. And then they rolled in, flying Trump banners, Confederate flags, blue and black American flags and the standard red, white and blue flag.

The march that day had begun in the courtyard of St. Barnabas Episcopal Church. And so had the idea for the march. But it was not a march led by the church. It was a community march. The church had merely opened its heart and grounds to the marchers. And that is how progressive Christians operate: open their doors to those who share their beliefs on the issues that face us right here on this earth.

As a political activist in New York, I've sat in meetings in the sanctuaries and meeting rooms of Lutheran, Presbyterian and Unitarian churches. These weren't church meetings. These are churches whose pastors and parishioners said yes when groups like the one I volunteer for — Empire State Indivisible — call and say, "May we use your meeting room?" These are churches that let the contemporary world around them come in, rather than trying to bar their doors to keep that world out.

And so it was with St. Barnabas Episcopal Church. It has a pretty little Mission-style building that evokes Spanish colonial churches, with its stucco facade and arched roof. Its current pastor, the Rev. Doug Bleyle, heard about St. Barnabas when he was attending the Iliff School of Theology in Denver in 2003. Father Doug comes from a family that counts four ordained Methodist minsters, including his father.

When he was growing up, some of the elders in his community told him: "You are going to fit in your father's shoes wonderfully." He wasn't convinced — although the church was central to his life. So he became an occupational therapist. But as I heard over and over from the activist people of faith I interviewed for this book, he kept feeling something tugging at him.

"Such things as calls to ministry eventually one cannot keep at bay," he wrote me in an email.

So, in 2003, while still working as an occupational therapist, he enrolled in the Iliff School of Theology, which is known for its strong social justice orientation. It was at Iliff that Father Doug first heard about St. Barnabas. It surprised him to hear about a small Episcopal church on Colorado's often-conservative Western Slope.

But it's not that surprising. Father Doug reminded me that the Episcopal Church has been a leader when it comes to adapting to the world it lives in. It began ordaining women as priests in the 1970s. It has welcomed the LGBTQ community since 1976 and stood firm in backing the LGBTQ community's equal protection under the law.

St. Barnabas comes from that tradition. Its former pastor, the Rev. Leigh Waggoner, once hosted a conversation group in which atheists, Buddhists, Episcopalians and others discussed national and world politics and events. The St. Barnabas website says the church welcomes everyone. It repeats the word "everyone" and underlines it on the second reference. There is a rainbow on its website. It trains facilitators for the Montezuma Youth Pride program, which meets both at the Montezuma-Cortez High School and the Cortez Middle School. Plus it hosts Youth Pride meetings in the church.

In August 2019, the church hosted a discussion entitled, "How You Can Be Part of a Christian Community with Integrity and Not Believe All Those Things You Thought You Had to Believe."[2] This is a Christian church that acknowledges doubt.

St. Barnabas was the incubator for the march that I

witnessed. A couple of its parishioners planted the seed for what became the Walk for Justice and Peace, a weekly event for about a year. Black Lives Matter is one of several issues for which these activists advocated. The group sought to put a spotlight on identity-based violence against all people, including the local Navajo and Ute populations, the Hispanic population and the LGBTQ community.

The Cortez marchers also acknowledged the expropriation of land from Indigenous people. They protested the unsolved deaths and disappearances of the Diné, the Navajo word for The People. And they protested the 2001 murder of 16-year-old Fred Martinez, a transgender Navajo youth, a two-spirit who would have been revered in earlier eras. But in 2001, he was beaten to death.

Again, this wasn't a St. Barnabas march. It was a community march that started each week in the church courtyard. Every Saturday starting in June 2020, marchers — only some of whom were part of the St. Barnabas congregation — gathered at St. Barnabas and then marched along Cortez's Main Street.

Sylvia Clahchischilli, a member of St. Barnabas, was among those who suggested taking to the street in this way, a proposal triggered by George Floyd's murder in May 2020.

Sylvia is Navajo. She takes the Navajo view of life as a journey. The journey's path is not always clear and there are often obstacles, but there are also helpers on this road.

Sylvia's mother raised her as Christian and Sylvia attended and enjoyed church services. That changed when her parents sent her to a Christian boarding school. She liked the teachers.

But the dorm parents were different.

"They were like a really bad stepmother, a really bad babysitter," she remembered. "Your parents trust that you will be cared for, and you are not." The staff was severely punitive. Sylvia recalled the time staff would not let one little girl to get out of bed to go to the bathroom before 6 a.m., the time kids were supposed to get up. So the child wet her bed.

The staff told the kids how they should speak and behave.

"A friend of mine described it as obtaining scalps for Christ," she said.

The dorm parents "were not loving people. They said God was loving, but they weren't," she said. "I didn't have a problem with God. We knew God, we knew a way of life, of what was in harmony, and love, all the things that Christians talk about, we knew it."

While in grad school in California, she attended an Episcopal church in Pasadena. . "And the priest was gay. And gay couples would come holding hands and that was new for me."

She loved it. She had long felt, as a Navajo operating in a white world, like an immigrant in her own land. All Saints showed her something different.

"To me it meant it was accepting of differentness. ... Here is this church, it's accepting," she said, and then added, "All Saints embodied who Jesus is, the one who was criticized and reprimanded by church leaders for associating with differentness."

She returned to the Navajo reservation, which stretches across Arizona, New Mexico, Utah and Colorado. And she was confirmed in the Episcopal church. She was also an activist, joining Diné Citizens Against Ruining the Environment, a grassroots organization that advocates justice for all creation, people and nature. "We celebrated a number of victories but also saw plenty of Indigenous protests unheeded," she said.

As years passed, she felt a lot of Native American protests just did not get the attention they deserved. And she saw the same happening with other minorities. And then came the hashtag Black Lives Matter, after a white man was acquitted in the shooting death of African American teen Trayvon Martin in 2013. Sylvia watched Black Lives Matter gain momentum.

"It's the genocide of the African American people, " she said. "They also were singing our prayer song. ... All of a sudden all these other groups, Hispanics, Native Americans, Asians, LGBTQ, we became this huge marginalized group."

Then a white Minneapolis policeman murdered George Floyd, a crime recorded in excruciating and undeniable detail on seventeen-year-old Darnella Frazier's cellphone.

The Sunday after George Floyd's death, Sylvia attended the St. Barnabas church service on Zoom and stayed on for the post-service virtual coffee hour. People talked about tasks for the soup kitchen, but not about George Floyd. And Sylvia was full of grief over Floyd's death plus all of those who have died for the wrong reason, and no reason.

A tiny voice whispered in her ear. Sylvia told me that the Navajo call this voice, *nilch'iyazhi.* It means little wind, spirit, breath. It is so quiet that it is more breath than whisper; she said. But it will not stop. We all hear that voice and, all too often, we ignore it. I think maybe it's the voice Father Doug heard before he started to attend Iliff.

Sylvia couldn't ignore the voice.

The voice kept pestering her.

"It was from George Floyd's death and all of those deaths that happened because of the color of their [the victims'] skin, it was all those deaths, but it came down to George Floyd, choking. It was very, very stark, in your face. I just couldn't leave it alone."

She and another parishioner contacted Father Doug. "What do you want to do?" he asked.

"I want to take it to the street," Sylvia said. Without hesitation, Father Doug replied, "I'll support you."

"It all started in two days," she said. "We had elders, young adults, children and babies in strollers."

Here's why St. Barnabas was such a natural for this. We've

seen that the Episcopal church ordained women and welcomed the LGBTQ community in the 1970s.

It was a little while coming, but in 2003, the Episcopal diocese of New Hampshire ordained its first openly gay bishop, Gene Robinson.[4]

A little more than a decade after that, the Episcopal Church took a hard look at race and how it played out within the church. In 2015 the Church elected Michael Curry its first presiding bishop of color. That is also when it examined how it had benefited from the economics of slavery and, in the present day, systemic racism. Several Episcopal dioceses have launched reparation programs. Among the biggest, the diocese of Texas, has said it is allocating $13 million to long-term programs for African Americans. These include scholarships for students attending seminaries or historically Black colleges and for Black churches.

So, St. Barnabas was a logical place for a march in support of Black Lives Matter in a community where there are few Blacks but plenty of Indigenous, Hispanic and Latinx people. Seventy people showed up the first Saturday. And only some were from the church. The turnout amazed Sylvia.

I imagine she must have been as thrilled as I was when I saw the marchers myself that September morning. There were a lot of young people. Young parents, with their kids in strollers.

The first few Saturdays, the march moved down Montezuma Avenue, a mostly residential street that is just half a block from the church and parallels Main Street, the town's main drag. After a few Saturdays the Justice and Peace marchers changed their route to Main Street.

The procession rapidly became a community-run event attracting people from throughout Cortez and the surrounding area. One of those newcomers was Raleigh Marmorstein.

Raleigh is someone who I believe is *perfect* for Montezuma

County. That's because she belies all sorts of stereotypes. Her father's father survived the Holocaust, and while her father was raised as a Jew, he attended Catholic school. He is not Catholic, but he loves Christmas and Jesus. Her mother is Catholic. So Raleigh grew up with both traditions and now considers herself is Jewish by blood (she did DNA testing) personal history and choice.

She's originally from southeast Michigan, outside of Detroit. This child of the Midwest grew up dreaming of the mountains. So after she earned her BS in psychology at Northern Michigan University, she headed west to Denver. She earned her EdS (education specialist) from the University of Denver. And then this enthusiastic snowboarder and hiker got an internship in Cortez.

Damn, I thought when she told me that — *you're living my dream!* Wisconsin, where I grew up and learned to ski, is just one state and one Great Lake over from Michigan. I started skiing out West when I was a freshman in college and decided to move to the West at some point. And I did, for a bit, spending one ski season in Aspen, Colorado, when I was in my 20s.

I ended up in New York City, but those mountains call me still. When I dragged my kids out West to see America and be with family, I also hoped they'd fall in love with the mountains. They did.

Mountain-loving Raleigh went to work in the home she'd chosen for herself and became a school psychologist at the San Juan Board of Cooperative Educational Services and is based in Cortez.

She met her husband on Match.com. He was working in Durango, just under fifty miles east of Cortez — and they got married in April 2021. Their wedding ceremony was on a mountaintop, on the San Sophia Overlook, near the San Sophia gondola in Telluride. The popular ski area is about seventy miles northeast of Cortez. Their wedding day was the kind of day that makes people fall hopelessly in love with the mountains, a sunny day with cloudless blue skies.

Before the Justice and Peace walks started, she hadn't been involved with St. Barnabas; now she's also a volunteer with the church food kitchen.

Another of the marchers was Dawn Robertson, an Americorps volunteer and a communications specialist for the local school district. She had moved to Cortez just five days before the marchers assembled for the first time in the St. Barnabas courtyard. Like Montezuma County itself, she embodies many cultures — daughter of a white mother and a Black man. She was raised by a Christian fundamentalist mother outside of Boston but is now Buddhist. She was a volunteer for the Democratic National Convention in 2012, and her experience in Montezuma County reminds her of something she was told when she was working at the Democratic National Convention.

"The Republican Party is run like a religion and attracts people who feel safe in a solidly paternalistic system run from the top down," she remembered her colleague telling her. She doesn't believe it fully defines the Republican Party, but it explains a lot about how it operates today.

Dawn estimated that at least two hundred different people have marched with the group since the Justice and Peace marches began.

Obviously, the marchers didn't go unnoticed.

In July, the counter-protests started. The counter-protestors were members of a group that calls itself the Montezuma County Patriots. Some folks in Montezuma County have a different name for them: Hatriots. I consider that accurate. Many of them carry guns. These counter protestors disrupted the downtown by driving big trucks, revving their engines, honking horns and waving the banners of the far right.

Over time, the counter-protestors became ever more aggressive. They left their trucks and moved to walking among the Justice and Peace marchers, weaving in and out of the group, spewing vitriol. One video shows a counter-protestor on foot harassing the peaceful marchers, swearing at them, telling them to go home. One of those he told to go home has lived in Cortez for more than forty years and is a veteran.

Early on, the marchers went to the police department and its brand new chief, Vernon Knuckles. He had just been sworn in as chief at the end of June 2020.

He met with the marchers at St. Barnabas. "They asked me to march with them," Vernon said. "I couldn't do that," he told me.

However, he told the marchers to call the department when they felt they needed help and said that, if the dispatcher did not seem to respond appropriately, to bump the call up to a supervisor.

As Vernon had promised, Cortez police officers responded to a call from marchers when the counter-protestors were walking around the marchers and swearing at them. The counter-protestors told the officer they were excising their right to free speech.

"But when you guys start swearing obscenities, that's a problem," one officer said to the counter-protestor, according to a story about the incident in *The Cortez Journal*. The counter-protestors continued their heckling, calling the marchers holding Black Lives Matter signs part of a terrorist organization. One counter-protestor said, "We're trying to run them out of town."

Another counter-protestor confronted a woman carrying a rainbow flag. "Are you gay? Are you gay?" he asked.

The police stayed with the marchers.

In another encounter, a right-wing counter-protestor told a

police officer he was trying to help the police. The policeman responded: "That's not your job, go home."

Vernon Knuckles is a contradictory guy. The new chief grew up in Egnar (range spelled backward), the small town that is the gateway to Disappointment Valley. Members of the Knuckles family have been in Montezuma County for generations. His Facebook page, which he has now taken down, featured shares of posts by others that defended the police, criticized the Black Lives Matter movement, and questioned policies about the Covid vaccine, one of which compared getting vaccinated to getting on trains to Nazi death camps.

That last one stunned me. The Nazis forcibly rounded up Jews and other victims and sent them to death camps where they were murdered methodically and brutally. There is no similarity between the Nazi assembly line killing the innocent and a health care system that created a vaccine in record time to save lives. Schools in this country have requires students to prove they're vaccinated against various diseases for *decades*. Every year, I rushed to my kids' doctor for documentation that my kids' vaccinations against chickenpox, diphtheria, hepatitis B, measles, mumps, pertussis (whooping cough) and tetanus (lockjaw) were up to date. The polio vaccine (remember that earlier pandemic?) was on that list, too. Ditto the meningitis B vaccine for most college students. An ounce of prevention really is worth a pound of cure. Or lifesaving.

But Vernon posted one link on his now-defunct Facebook page showing that professionalism is important to him. It was a link to an article he wrote for the FBI Law Enforcement Bulletin about leadership. Vernon wrote in the post that he was honored to have it published. He wrote the article while he was an undersheriff for the Montezuma County sheriff's department; it's a solid and well-written piece about developing talent.

Vernon also attended the FBI National Academy in Quantico, Virginia. He is justifiably proud of that accomplishment. Perhaps that commitment to professionalism is why he appears to leave his politics at home when he goes to work as chief of police.

When I asked him about his Facebook posts, he said he had made a mistake in sharing those posts. When I was still able to look at his Facebook page, I also found posts about a pushup contest for charity and a few about an aesthetician business (his wife is an aesthetician). He also pointed out that his posts were infrequent and spread out over several years. And he also posted them, he said, to give an alternate point of view.

Initially, he resisted taking the posts down.

"I told everyone, 'I'm not going to take it down because I don't want to be accused of hiding,'" he told me. Now, I understand that idea of owning up to your mistakes. On the other hand, people like the far-right counter-protestors must have read those and seen him as their ally. But ultimately, he shut down his entire Facebook page. He said it was just too much of a firestorm to be worth it.

"As a human being, I think he walks honestly," one of the Justice and Peace marchers told me. "It feels like working with him, he sets his politics aside as much as anyone can."

He's been straightforward with me in describing the intransigence of the right-wing counter-protestors.

Those counter-protestors planned a 100-truck rally the Saturday before the November 2020 election, suggesting to participants that they "pack with pride." This was to be a Second Amendment event.

Cortez Mayor Mike Lavey became concerned. Mike is a surprise for anyone who looks at electoral maps. He's a Democrat. He's the Democratic mayor of the city that is the county seat in a county that *looks* really red. And he's part of a determined progressive movement, something you'll find across the nations in other counties that look really red, but aren't. He had worked hard to build bridges between opposing groups in Cortez.

With the pre-election 100-truck rally in mind, the mayor called the police chief.

"I'm going to be there," Mike said to Vernon.

Vernon reached out to one of the main organizers.

"They were calling for everybody to bring their guns and come down on Main Street and march around," the police chief told me. "I said, 'You know, this is a horrible idea. There's nothing good to come out of it.'"

"You came to support, to back the blue," he recalled telling one of the group's organizers, "but everything you're doing is costing resources and it's causing us problems. And to me, that's not supporting law enforcement." I thought that was a great thing for the police chief to say to someone ostensibly supporting police.

The group canceled the rally, although Vernon said a lot of group members did not want to.

But that wasn't the end of it. As January 6 and the congressional vote to formally ratify the Electoral College results approached, the Patriots revved up. Saturday, January 2, more than a dozen Patriots circled and harassed five Justice and Peace demonstrators.

I watched a video of the incident.[3]

It's ugly. Really ugly.

The five Justice and Peace participants weren't marching. They stood on a corner of Main Street, simply holding signs. As always, they had cleared their activity with the police department. Then, when the counter-protestors descended upon them, they approached from two directions. They waved the flags of the far right, blue and black versions of the American flag, a Colorado for Trump flag (featuring both a Colorado state flag and an American flag), and Trump 2020 flags.

They stood within inches of the Justice and Peace demonstrators, and taunted and cursed them. "Fuck you!," "Fuck Black Lives Matter," "All lives matter, bitch," "Get down on your knees." One talked about showing up on Raleigh Marmorstein's doorstep and noted that the police were driving past the hecklers without doing anything. They called the Justice and Peace demonstrators Nazis. The demonstrators did not respond to the harassers, but in the video you can hear them checking in with each other to see if they were comfortable with staying or if they wanted to return to the church earlier than planned. The group stuck it out.

Then, as the Justice and Peace participants walked toward St. Barnabas, the right-wing group followed them, peppering them with insults. Raleigh, who was using her phone to video the right-wing group, asked another demonstrator to call Father Doug, to warn him that the church might have to prepare for trespassers. The right-wing group stopped at the entryway to the churchyard, with a few people suggesting the group go on in. They lingered at the gate, discussed walking into the courtyard, but then drifted away.

Because of that video, six members of the right-wing group now face harassment charges in Montezuma County Combined Courts.

The mayor, Mike Lavey, was nearby. He'd been keeping an eye on the Justice and Peace group, and the right-wingers then descended upon him. Mike told me the group surrounded him, shouting at him and calling him a commie and a socialist.

These name callers did not know their man. Besides being mayor and a Navy veteran who served overseas, Mike has worked as a courtroom security officer and is a former special deputy with the Montezuma County sheriff's department. In the Navy, he trained in the use of rifles and handguns, and he got additional firearms instruction when training for the special deputy position some years ago. That's also when he first learned how to use tasers. When the trainer asked for a volunteer to be hit by a taser, Mike offered to take the hit, literally.

"It's 50,000 watts," he said. "It is crippling. You cannot move at all. It hits all the muscle groups." Not only does he know how to *use* a taser, he knows *why* it's so effective.

On January 6, as rioters were smashing windows of our nation's Capitol, assaulting police and trying to break down doors to seize members of Congress, the right-wing counter-protestors, many of them armed, convened again in downtown Cortez for about three hours. Although they verbally attacked anyone who walked by, they stayed in one spot.

I've talked to the police chief a lot about his vision for his job. Dealing with right-wing counter-protestors was not what Vernon Knuckles had in mind when he became police chief. His initial goal was to institute community policing, using the guiding principles of Sir Robert Peele, who was twice prime minister of England and was the guy who established the London police force. You know, the cops who don't carry guns. Even today. Only specially trained authorized firearm officers (AFOs) carry guns in London. Peele is considered the father of modern policing. His principles were the core of President Obama's task force on law enforcement, Vernon told me in an email.

"If you can make your way through that," he said, hinting that he might have found it to be a dense read. Or perhaps he's not an Obama fan.

Peele's principles are about *preventing* crime, *not* catching criminals, which flies in the face of the stereotypical image of American policing, you know, cops chasing robbers. And the fact that this was Vernon's philosophy of law enforcement surprised me. He'd wanted to be a cop from the age of eight when a relative who worked for the sheriff's department in Sacramento, California, took him on a night-shift ride-along.

He's been in law enforcement for most of his adult life. He started with the Montezuma County sheriff's department, then worked as a ranger for Colorado State Parks while attending the police academy at the Technical College of the Rockies and then went to work for the Cortez Police Department. He joined the National Guard, then served sixteen months with the Army in Iraq and later returned to Iraq with a job protecting diplomats.

A lot of what he told me about Iraq sounds like something out of a war movie. Vernon was a platoon sergeant leading a Humvee escort of a convoy coming in with supplies from Kuwait. Insurgents ambushed the convoy halfway across a bridge. Vernon, in the lead vehicle, with his machine gunner and grenadier, fought back firing machine guns and launching grenades, ultimately killing the attackers, only to come under sniper fire. He got a Bronze Star for that one, for saving lives and millions of dollars of mission-critical supplies.

There were long days of clearing roads, disarming IEDs — either blowing them up or cutting the wires or both. There were days working with Sunnis and coming under attack by Shiites and vice versa in a country torn by religious factions. And I thought to myself, *This is what I don't want to happen here!*

Vernon came home from that tour to divorce and debt and, a year later, in 2003, went back to Iraq, this time working for a military contractor providing security for diplomats.

Baghdad was like the Wild West. "At any given time you could hear scrimmages, bombs, stuff going off. You could hear rocket fire at one end of the city and in another, mortars and small arms." His job was to escort diplomatic staff to meetings around the city, meetings that might come under attack.

"Our primary mission was to get the protected party out of there, not to stay and fight." They'd hustle the officials out, sometimes firing at attackers just long enough to get the hell out of Dodge. Vernon was there until about 2008 — ninety days on duty, thirty days stateside, for five years.

"You were there five years?" I said. "You must've liked it."

"It was awesome," he replied.

He's still in the National Guard.

Working toward a community policing model is still his goal. It's hard, for economic reasons — Cortez is not a rich city in the best of times — as well as for cultural. When I interviewed him in April 2021, Vernon had just gotten the department's quarterly report. The top event category was domestic violence and assault summonses. Violations of restraining orders also ranked high in that report.

Vernon has reached out to the Justice and Peace marchers for help with a new project he is initiating, a community intervention program involving a special unit staffed by a mental health clinician and an EMT (emergency medical technician) They'll respond to calls for service that are unrelated to crime, like emotional health crises. Or if, for example, someone is threatening suicide and has locked himself or herself into a bedroom with a knife, police will respond —with the mental health clinician. These are incidents that can require a police officer's presence for hours, but mental health is not the officer's core expertise at all. It'll take some training; dispatchers will have to determine how to appropriately route incoming calls.

The community intervention program will operate separately from either the police and sheriff's department. Vernon said that having police involved might make some people in Cortez reluctant to call for help. He talked to Raleigh about the program, and she immediately agreed that she and her group will help in whatever way they can. The program has funding now, but at some point Vernon anticipates having to go to voters to get approval for more funding. So he's working on getting the community behind the initiative now.

He's got other ideas. Police often offer to help homeless people, especially in the winter. But many homeless people don't want to take shelter, so Vernon envisions a partnership in the community where local churches, which already work with the homeless, can provide police with warm clothes for the homeless who refuse shelter. At the Colorado Association of Chiefs of Police annual conference in June, he heard a presentation from the group Faith in Blue. One of its main organizers is the Rev. Markel Hutchins, a human and civil rights leader and activist. When I read about the group, I was psyched. *This is the way to involve the clergy, especially progressive clergy and clergy in communities of color, with police.* It is an idea that fills me with both hope and excitement and it seems to me that some of what Vernon is trying to set up fits in with this model.

I asked Vernon how he thought people could work together in today's political climate. I thought his vantage point as a police chief in a small town in southwestern Colorado would be helpful.

"I just feel that you have to communicate," he said. Then he surprised me: "I think a barrier to some of the communication we've seen is mostly on the Patriot side," referring to the far-right group that calls people names and swears at them. What that group calls communication, he said, seemed to him to be "trying to change minds and bring the other side into their side."

But, I wanted to make sure that I had heard him correctly when he talked about the right-wing counter-protestors. So I asked him a follow-up question, inviting him to essentially repeat himself.

"Do you think both sides are doing that?"

"I see it more on the Patriot side," he said, again referring to the right-wing group. "And that just, that causes walls to be built, you know, they're defensive and you just don't get anything done. I'm not here to change anybody's minds. I'm not, you know, I'm not for either side. I just want to make sure both sides are allowed to do what they're allowed to do under the Constitution."

He went on to say that he tries to bring up whatever concerns he has with both sides.

"And I'll tell you," he said, "the hardest conversations I've had to have are with the Patriots."

I like Vernon although some of what I saw on his Facebook page discomfited me. But, given I grew up in a reddish-purple corner of the state of Wisconsin, I'm used to having friends whose views worry me. So, I can be concerned about some of the posts he shared on Facebook and still believe that he is a straightforward and honest guy.

We talked about running — he had run the Marine Marathon in Washington, D.C. — and it had nearly killed him. I told him I had run the Imogene Pass Run from Ouray, Colorado, to Telluride, Colorado, and it nearly killed me, too. So we talked about that. We clearly disagree about a lot, but we agree on some things. Most importantly, we can talk to each other. And that's what this nation needs a lot more of. A helluva lot more of.

The police chief and the mayor seem to have a civil relationship when it comes to dealing with the problems Cortez is facing, but it's the mayor who takes the heat from right wingers. A lot of it is because he's a Democrat. And some of it is because he's lived in Cortez for "only" a little more than thirty years.

The mayor has been viciously targeted by the right wing in person, as evidenced by the January 2 incident, and in social media. Gail, his wife, has been targeted as well. One right-wing counter-protestor speaking at a city council meeting falsely accused Gail of spraying the right-winger with wasp spray during a Justice and Peace march. Gail countered that she had not been at the march, and the right-winger then apologized.

Nobody had sprayed anything on anyone. Making false accusations is typical for this group — although in this instance, the person making such accusations got caught and had to apologize. Telling lies about people is a classic intimidation tactic, and intimidation is standard procedure for the right-wing counter-protestors in Cortez.

Raleigh, for example, agreed to meet with two members of her group at a cafe the group considers its territory. Once seated at a table with the friends, at least two other people paced around her, Glocks at their hips. Raleigh introduced herself to one woman who responded brusquely, "I know who you are." That was it. Later that woman texted Raleigh, "I should have said, 'I'll pray for you.'"

After Raleigh told me that, I could hear Uncle Zel—the uncle who'd teased my siblings and me as little kids with his mock holiness routine—chortling over that one. I think he would have worked it into his comedy routine.

The Cortez right-wingers get even more virulent on Facebook, writing lies that are both defamatory and filled with hate. I'm not repeating those lies, nor am I naming the perpetrators because I think they crave attention. Mike is a stark contrast to this group, thoughtful, courageous and honest. He strives to build bridges between people, not walls. He has brought opposing groups into city council meetings to provide an organized forum for people to express their opinions.

Mike has been mayor just a little longer than Vernon has been chief of police. As noted, he's lived in Cortez for more than thirty years; he raised his family there. Years before moving to Cortez, Mike served in the U.S. Navy. He was on shore patrol duty in 1962 during the Cuban Missile Crisis and spent forty days in a ship circling Cuba.

One of my high school classmates was in grade school in Florida at the time. Kids had daily drills to hide under their desks in case of attack. Armageddon loomed.

"After everybody stepped down and there was no nuclear holocaust after all, we all went to our port," Mike said. "All the sailors and all the Marines were let off the ship and went to an NCO Club."

And in that NCO (noncommissioned officers) Club, those sailors and Marines let go a global amount of steam and tension, he recalled.

The place exploded.

There is nothing like a fight in a bar packed with soldiers back from a high-stakes operation. They are primed to blow up. I saw one big one when I was tending bar at the NCO Club at Fort McCoy, back in Wisconsin.

It was right out of an old Western. There was the buzz of music, conversation and laughter — and then, a couple of guys jumped up, knocking chairs and tables over. I heard the sharp sound of glass shattering. Men punched and wrestled with each other. Others tried to pull them apart. There was shouting and swearing. A guy standing at the bar said to me, "Stay back there," (no way was I going to leave!) and then dove into the fray.

The fight spread like wildfire throughout the entire bar — which was the size of my high school gym. So much was happening it was hard to keep track of it. Then the military police (MPs) stormed in, blowing whistles, pulling soldiers off each other.

Mike was patrolling a crowd like that in the Florida NCO club. But he was shore patrol, not an MP. He faced the brawling crowd with nothing more than a billy club and a little armband that said SP. Little did he know how that experience would prepare him for being mayor of a small town he had never heard of.

After he left the Navy, Mike earned a degree in comparative literature at UC Riverside. He met his wife, Gail, who was an English major, when both were working for a local bookmobile.

As they began raising their family — they have two kids — the two decided they did not want to stay in California. On a vacation, they fell in love with Colorado's Western Slope. Mike, who was working with the U.S. Postal Service, got a transfer to Cortez. Gail worked as a librarian in a local elementary school.

They just celebrated their 40th wedding anniversary.

The 2016 election changed the couple's world.

"I never thought I would be a precinct organizer for the Democratic Party. I never thought I would be a city council member, much less mayor!" Mike told me.

In 2016, Mike and Gail had been attending an evangelical church. But after the 2016 election, after 80 percent of evangelicals had voted for Trump, they quit that church.

"I was so displeased and angered," he said.

He started going to Democratic Party meetings and someone suggested he run for city council.

"Impossible," Mike said.

But he ran and was the third-highest vote getter. In his campaign marketing materials, he used a photo of himself in a suit. He went door to door and talked to Democrats and Republicans alike. It probably helped that he had been a mail carrier in town for years. It also helped that term limits opened up seats on the council. Then, in April 2020, other council members voted him in as mayor. He has worked hard to try to build bridges between opposing factions.

Although Mike and Gail attended an evangelical church, they also worked on the food pantry at St. Barnabas. It didn't matter that they worshipped elsewhere. The two were on the board of the food kitchen. After the 2016 election, Mike called the then-pastor, Rev. Leigh Waggoner, for consolation.

The 2016 election was even more disturbing for Gail than it had been for her husband. She described it as an existential crisis.

Gail had, in her words, accepted Jesus through the Campus Crusade for Christ while in college. Mike had been raised Catholic, but Gail was the driving force, religiously speaking, for the couple.

She was deeply involved in the conservative church they had belonged to. She had been a deacon, worked in the Sunday school, helped with vacation Bible school and led Bible studies.

"I was hook, line and sinker for a long, long time," she told me when I interviewed her in December 2020.

Then came the 2016 election.

"They backed Trump in our own little church," she said. "These are the people who are our people and they are supporting Trump. These are not our people."

Looking back, she said there was a gradual shift in her church.

"I don't know when it changed. I just floated along with it in my own naive little world thinking we were about Jesus and going and helping our neighbor and getting closer to God," she recalled.

"And all of a sudden, I'm going, wait a minute, this is not it."

Gail felt she needed a break from religion.

Then, her husband heard of the United Methodist Church in the town of Mancos, only twenty minutes east of Cortez.

Mancos Methodist has the same kind of deliberative approach to issues that St. Barnabas has. When the global United Methodist Church began talking about how to handle LGBTQ issues (see chapter 6 for more on that) Mancos Methodist had a meeting.

"In our church we started having a discussion about that

before the bigger church told us what would happen," its minister, the Rev. Craig Paschal, told me.

"We brought in the parents of gay children and members of our own congregation to talk about their experiences and [to] educate ourselves," he said.

And Mancos Methodist became what it describes as a reconciling church. "We publicly proclaim everyone is welcome and that we accept all people regardless of sexual orientation and gender identification. We are all made in God's image and are loving children with God. ...

"And not only are they welcome but [so are] other groups that have been marginalized." Once the church did that, "a weight lifted off us," Paschal said.

Inertia is a powerful force. And Mancos Methodist fought it.

"We stand firm with the radical love of Christ," he said.

Hmm. What's radical for a Methodist? I wondered.

Well, in the American West, Methodist radical can mean making a gay minister your bishop. The bishop of the Methodist Western Jurisdiction Conference, Mountain Sky Episcopal Area, Karen Oliveto, is gay. And, she is married.

Then Paschal told me something else.

Repent, he said, means to have a new mind, a new consciousness.

Did you know that? I didn't! I thought it meant pounding your chest and telling God and the world how awful you are and how you deserve to be punished.

He didn't call his church progressive. He called it "Christ centered."

"It's pretty straightforward. Love your neighbor. Love your enemy."

Love. That word keeps coming up with these progressive, er, Christ-centered types. And that seemed to lead quite logically to the next step for Mancos Methodist. After the 2016 election, someone, and Paschal cannot remember who it was, asked, "Why aren't we a sanctuary church?"

In one church discussion, a woman asked, "How can we call ourselves a church if we don't love our neighbor?"

Paschal learned that members of fifteen families in Mancos — a town of 1,400 — were at risk of deportation. All the families had been in the area for ten years or more. That startled Paschal. These were people who had children in local schools, who dated others in the community, who visited each other's homes for dinner. In a town as small as Mancos, everyone knows everyone.

Paschal signed up the church for a two-day sanctuary training through the Methodist church in early 2017. He learned that, at the time, there were only eight people in the whole country being protected in sanctuary churches.

"We thought it wouldn't happen," he said.

They thought wrong.

In May, someone who is Catholic but comes to the Methodist church after going to Mass, emailed Paschal.

A woman who had lived in Mancos for thirty years faced deportation.

Her name is Isabel Sabido. She worked for the Catholic church writing newsletters and ran a small business selling homemade tamales. For the past several years, she had requested stays of deportation from federal immigration authorities. In the spring of 2017, she learned that her latest request had been denied.

Church members discussed the situation, then made their decision.

"We just said, 'We can do this,'" said Rev. Paschal. "It was rooted in the basic premise in loving your neighbor, loving the stranger."

An entire community has sprung up to support Isabel,

providing her with physical and emotional sustenance, taking tamale cooking lessons from her and participating in political campaigns to help her and others like her.

In life, I've found, it's often two steps forward and one step back. And Montezuma County recently took a step back — when the right-wingers went after Santa Claus.

Picture Santa wearing jeans and a tie-dyed T-shirt driving an eighteen-wheeler instead of a sleigh. That's Lance McDaniel. His long white beard makes him a natural for playing Santa Claus for charities at Christmas (in 2020 it was virtual). Born and raised in Cortez, he left after high school and returned a few years ago. He jumped back into the community, volunteering with a shelter for domestic violence, and becoming a member of groups including Moms Demand Gun Sense and a group called Montezuma Lands for Unity.

He participated when Montezuma Lands for Unity and pastors from Cortez and Mancos churches — St. Barnabas, Mancos Methodist and First United Methodist of Cortez — held a vigil after a mass shooting. He took a child abuse prevention course offered by the Four Corners Child Advocacy Center and, before he became a member of the school board, suggested that all members of the school board take the class as well.

"They did not take kindly to that," he said.

Long an advocate for public education, he landed a position on the school board when a vacancy opened up. He then became part of an anti-human trafficking task force. At some point, he started helping St. Barnabas Church deliver pizzas to the Rainbow Clubs, Friday lunch clubs held for LGBTQ kids at the middle school, high school and charter school. He'd drive the pizzas to the schools and hand them over to an on-site teacher. Then, in October 2019, he met a few of the kids.

"I told them I was a board member, I told them what board members do and promised to always fight for them," he said.

The kids told him how wonderful it was to have one place once a week to be safe. He wrote about the experience on Facebook.

This posting and other evidence of Lance's worldview triggered an anti-Lance movement. His critics found their opening and leapt on a clumsy joke he had made about veterans in a light-hearted exchange with three friends — two former Marines and one Navy vet — on Facebook. The joke bombed. (In his Twitter bio, he describes himself as "Sarcastic. Funny sometimes.")

"We were joking, and me, not knowing some people actually stalk people on Facebook, I was having a smartass exchange with veteran friends that was taken seriously by some of the people," he said.

Lance's right-wing neighbors were gunning for him and sooner or later would have found an excuse to go after him. By July 2020, the right-wingers were aiming to oust him from the school board. A recall petition said Lance "had shown a lack of leadership and has proven to be a poor role model for our children." The petition cited that joke about veterans.

Then, the school board held its October 2020 meeting. It was a hybrid meeting; people could attend in person or attend on Zoom.

The Montezuma right wing is a powder keg that can mobilize with lightning speed on Facebook. One right-winger made a Facebook post telling friends that anyone could attend the board meeting on Zoom. The post said something to the effect of "let's all go and let Lance know what we think."

Lance and a few board members were discussing some other issue when suddenly five or six Zoom attendees started talking — participants could mute or unmute themselves at will. In the recording, one person could be heard saying, "If you [unintelligible] one more time, I'm going to rape all of your daughters."

The school district went to the police, but no charges have been filed.

On February 16, 2021, three thousand voters turned out for a special election that cost the taxpayers of Montezuma County $21,000. They ousted Lance McDaniel two-to-one.

But that's just one part of Montezuma County. There's another part, and that part showed up at the May 25, 2021, meeting of the Cortez City Council. It unanimously approved declaring June Gay Pride Month in Cortez. About thirty people attended the meeting in person; others (including me) attended via Zoom. Four speakers praised the measure. Two speakers opposed it. Both are among those facing harassment charges for their treatment of the Justice and Peace marchers. I am not naming these right wingers because this chapter is about the heroes of Montezuma County.

One speaker, who actually lives several miles outside of Cortez, wore a black T-shirt with the word "Jesus" emblazoned on it in giant letters (when I saw that, I immediately wondered *Does she think Jesus is near-sighted?* and thought of how my Uncle Zel, with his unerring eye for sanctimonious unctuousness, would have applauded that). First she prayed (and my Uncle Zel would have *loved* this inappropriate invoking of God). Then, she told the LGBTQ community to "stop wanting to be considered equal." She wound up by saying that Cortez was risking the wrath of the God who, she said, destroyed Sodom and Gomorrah for its homosexual practices.

Except, of course, the Biblical story of Sodom and Gomorrah didn't explicitly mention homosexuality until a mid-twentieth century update (in English) of the Bible. For hundreds of years before that, that passage warned about excess and worship of false gods. (An observant Jewish friend told me that homosexuality is mentioned in the Hebrew version of the Old Testament, but it's one of a long list of sins of excess and probably was a reaction to Roman bacchanals, those hours-long parties that featured lavish food, entertainment, prostitutes and a lot of other excesses that might have looked pretty tempting to some people).

Just a reminder, 70 percent of Americans favor same-sex marriage. That speaker's cruel and hateful condemnation of the entire LGBTQ community is the exception, not the rule.

Another speaker, Rebecca Busick, spoke lovingly of her late brother-in-law, Mike Busick. "I am here," she said, "to honor his love and that of his husband, David, his partner of twenty years." She thanked the council for its vote and Mayor Mike Lavey for signing the proclamation.

"Discrimination has no place here or anywhere else. Love is love," she said. And then she added, "I hope other elected officials in this area follow your lead in taking a more inclusive approach to leadership."

Matt Kefauver, a former member of the city council and principal of the Southwest Open School in Cortez, also praised the proclamation.

"The past year has been full of a lot of hateful rhetoric, bullying and even threats to LGBTQ people and their allies. I believe that signing the proclamation could be the first step in healing a divided community," he said.

Raleigh Marmorstein also spoke. She praised the proclamation and called it "suicide prevention."

The proclamation declared Cortez a city that welcomes all, regardless of ethnicity, race, religion, gender identification, sexual orientation, age, profession, physical attributes or national origin. All people, including families of every shape, "deserve a place to call home, where they feel safe, happy and supported by friends and neighbors."

It also acknowledged that the city of Cortez lies on "unceded Ute and Pueblo land, the violent colonization of which includes cultural destruction and the forced assimilation and the deliberate and targeted punishment and erasure of Indigenous people."

The town of Mancos also declared June Gay Pride Month.

The Justice and Peace marchers ended their walks on the one-year mark. They are focusing on community work: helping the homeless, strengthening the group's ties with Indigenous people, and working with local law enforcement and educators about social justice and that new hot-button topic, critical race theory. I was in Cortez the weekend of Juneteenth and attended services at St. Barnabas on a sunny Sunday morning. The sanctuary was bright; sunshine filtered through stained-glass windows and illuminated golden oak pews. Sylvia Clahchischilli, who was among the first to suggest what became the Walk for Justice and Peace, met me outside and we went into the service together.

Father Doug talked about Paul's difficulties with the Corinthians. Paul is in conflict with the church in Corinth, which seems to have rejected his message and his work (it's rough being an apostle). He's trying to justify himself to them to win them back. He wants to hang on to the grace of God, the source of his energy — although the people of Corinth are rejecting his work. Paul starts talking about *skubalon,* an ancient Greek word meaning material to be disposed of — garbage, manure, excrement, kitchen scraps.

"I consider everything as lost because of the surpassing greatness of knowing Christ Jesus my Lord for the sake of whom I have suffered everything and considered it *skubalon* so that I might gain Christ." (Phil.3:8).

In a word, shit.

Basically, Paul is saying *skubalon* happens. Good things and bad things happen to you, often at the same time.

"Maybe," Father Doug said with a smile, "we could use this for fundraising; a bumper sticker that says, '*Skubalon* Happens.'"

I'll buy it.

It's perfect for Montezuma County. And our nation. And the world.

---

[1] "Politics & Voting in Cortez, Colorado." *Best Places. https://www.bestplaces.net/voting/city/colorado/cortez*

[2] "St. Barnabas Aug. 13 examines how we value education." *The Journal. https://www.the-journal.com/articles/st-barnabas-aug-13-gathering-examines-how-we-value-education/*

[3] Facebook https://www.facebook.com/1248270310/videos/pcb.10217855790726944/10217855700004676

10

PROGRESSIVE CHRISTIANITY: NOT AN OXYMORON

Churches throughout the nation are stepping up to the challenge of fighting for justice and truth today. A lot of us don't see that activism, in part because much of the mainstream media continue to let the sanctimonious loudmouths of the Republican right frame the conversation.

Partly it's because so many of us have bought into the way the right has branded religion as Christian nationalism.

Meet a few of the voices challenging that.

The Rev. Gina Gerbasi is rector of St. John's Church across Lafayette Square from the White House. This Episcopal church was the setting for President Trump's disastrous photo op on June 1, 2020. Riot police, some on the ground wearing helmets and carrying shields, some on horseback, chased peaceful demonstrators out of Lafayette Square. Police also set off explosions and fired sting balls and gas into the peaceful crowd. Photos and video showed demonstrators running away from the square. Clouds of smoke obscured the scene at times.

Then, site cleared, Trump walked through a gauntlet of armed police to the church, where he awkwardly held a Bible for the photo.

Rev. Gerbasi was there. She had been on St. John's patio, which had become a refuge and an aid station for demonstrators. She'd been handing out water to demonstrators when riot police descended upon her, chasing her from her own church.

Shortly after the incident, she talked about her experience in an interview on *Unholier Than Thou*. This was a podcast produced by Crooked Media, originators of *Pod Save America*, whose politically savvy (they're former Obama staffers) and bitingly funny hosts have had some fun remembering times when Democratic candidates have clumsily tried to assert that God guides them.

In that podcast. she told host Phillip Picardi about her anger. She was coldly angry about the way Trump subverted her church and I think she epitomized the anger driving many Christians who are outraged at how the right has co-opted Christianity. Gerbasi trained first as a lawyer and had to overcome a lot of interior resistance in order to become a priest — it sounds as though one part of her dragged the other part of her kicking and screaming into the holy orders.

I think it was that same voice that Sylvia Clahchischilli heard, the *nilch'iyazhi*. Gerbasi described those conversations as talking with God, who, she said, has a sense of humor. Hey, I like that!

She also talked about the sermon she preached — using video technology — on the Pentecost Sunday just before the June 1 incident. In the sermon, she talked about the way the Holy Spirit was given to God's people. It wasn't something delivered by some sweet choir of angels.

"It was a big wind with tongues of fire," Gerbasi told Picardi.

And then she added, "The Holy Spirit is here now, and she be pissed off." She talked about the large numbers of people demonstrating across the nation. "That is what the Holy Spirit looks like when she is unleashed," she said.

Here is what I find rare. Invoking God, the Holy Spirit or Jesus outside the church setting was something mainstream white clergy in my experience just didn't do. Bringing Jesus into daily life and public policy debates used to be mostly confined to conservative clergy. In fact, some members of that group have been pretty shameless about politicizing God. One caveat—as far back as the 1925 Scopes trial, which put the teaching of evolution in public schools on trial—Black preachers and writers have distanced themselves from white evangelicals. "They already knew how to be an evangelical and an American interested in progress,"[1] wrote Mary Beth Mathews in *Black Perspectives,* the African American Intellectual History Society's award-wing blog. They also believed Christians practiced equality and love, she wrote. Black churches, of course, power Souls to the Polls voter registration drives and voting and have been doing so for fifty years[2]. Republicans in states like Georgia are targeting these Sunday voter drives with voter suppression laws that eliminate early voting.

Unlike white evangelicals and activist Black clergy, mainstream clergy were more likely to keep church and state separate. Yes, they'd put parables and scripture into modern context when speaking from the pulpit. They didn't hesitate to join demonstrations either. But it was the Falwells and the Grahams you'd see on the news invoking Jesus's support of the right-wing Republican agenda. That's been changing as progressively minded activist clergy use Jesus' name and passages from the Bible to support helping refugees, as well as fighting racism, sexism and poverty.

Gerbasi sees the Holy Spirit flying over the nation and the world, energizing protestors. She's an Episcopalian — not the stereotyped Holy Roller preacher. She's talking about God, Jesus and social justice. I don't know if she's ever been to the Wild Goose Festival, but she would fit right in.

Other churches are fighting fire with fire by applying religious precepts to the politics of the day.

Two major issues moving people of faith to speak up: immigration and LGBTQ rights. One example: the Evangelical Lutheran Church of America. This is a mainline Protestant denomination, with about four million members and ten thousand congregations across the United States, which declared its entire denomination as a sanctuary in August 2019, proclaiming that "walking alongside immigrants and refugees is a matter of faith."[1] The denomination also said that it allows for LGBTQ marriage and ordination of LGBTQ clergy.

There are other big denominations that stood up to Trump when he tried to claim them as his own, including the Roman Catholic Church. Archbishop Jerome Listecki of Milwaukee learned that the "Catholics for Trump" campaign had scheduled its launch event in Milwaukee, in March 2020. Listecki basically said "Whoa!" He said the Catholic Church was "in no way affiliated to or sponsoring this event or campaign, locally, statewide or nationally." He unequivocally disassociated the church from the campaign.[3]

The Rev. William Barber is co-chair of the Poor People's Campaign, a new iteration of a movement begun by Dr. Martin Luther King, Jr. and others in 1968. The campaign advocates for the 140 million poor and low-income people in our country, who are found among people every race, creed, sexuality and place. When it comes to sheer numbers, there are more poor white people than poor Black people, he pointed out. The poor in America are as diverse as the nation itself.

Barber doesn't fight just poverty. He fights voter suppression. He fights the terrible things being done at our borders when our own government takes children from their parents and holds children and adults in conditions that some experts have described as akin to torture. Barber painted a picture of an activist Jesus. He said in a sermon in 2017 that Jesus died for our sins but was executed for sedition.[4] Sedition means conduct or speech that incites people to rebel against a state or monarch.

I heard the Rev. Barber speak at the Wild Goose Festival in July 2019. He is the kind of preacher who loves to whip up a crowd and he did that when I listened to him that day under the hot North Carolina sun. He said the Holy Spirit revives us and unites us. He invoked the Holy Spirit to help fight the forces that cause poverty, that cause racism, forces that fan the flames of hate and xenophobia. There were probably five hundred of us in the crowd, and all of us were on our feet, including me (to my astonishment), cheering the Holy Spirit, calling for a moral Pentecost in America "right here, right now," over and over.

I half expected armed and masked guerrilla fighters of the religious right to come swinging out of the surrounding trees to thwart us. I thought the revolution was starting right there, right then.

I had to look up the definition of the word Pentecost. It's basically the start of a mission to change the world.

Mainstream churches haven't stood alone in opposing Trumpism and the far right. Some church leaders who opposed Trump's policies came from the fabled Trump core. I am talking Southern Baptists, the cornerstone of Trump's base. These evangelical leaders protested —and some still are— Trump policies, using religion as justification for their opposition.

The policy that drove members of this group to protest: the Trump and Republican stance on immigration and the way the Trumpers handled the refugees at our border. Refugees were sleeping on concrete floors, with lights on 24/7.

"This is unconscionable," Dan Darling, vice president for communications at the Southern Baptist Convention's Ethics and Religion Commission, said in 2019.[5]

I mentioned earlier (chapter 5) that Galen Carey, the vice

president of government relations for the National Association of Evangelicals, told Congress that the U.S. refugee resettlement program is "the crown jewel of American humanitarianism." That was in 2017.[6] He opposed the religious litmus test for refugees. He stood up for immigrants and how they benefit America. And he reaffirmed the security of programs that vet refugees before they arrive.

The positions taken by these evangelical leaders have not dissolved the Trump core and they never will. They will, however, chip away at the edges, and that is what we need to build a coalition of the devout and the secular to promote social justice.

Some evangelicals actively chipped away at those edges during the 2020 presidential campaign.

Not Our Faith is a bipartisan super PAC that ran pro-Biden ads targeting Christian voters in key battleground states. One of the group's co-founders, Autumn Hanna VandeHei, was raised as an evangelical and has spent most of her career in Republican politics. She calls herself unabashedly pro-life. But, in an NPR interview just before the 2020 election, she said she recognizes that being pro-life is about far more than abortion, which she opposes.

She told NPR's Rachel Martin that abortion "shouldn't be the defining factor when we have so many other things at stake." Joe Biden has even said he is anti-abortion but still pro-choice. Abortion does not have to be the deal breaker political pundits and right-wingers make it out to be.

VandeHei made a point that a lot of commentators miss. There are plenty of pro-lifers who recognize that being pro-life is a package, not a concept limited to the abortion issue. I have heard this over and over from devout Americans who truly are guided by their religion, and they can challenge clergy who tell their parishioners to be single-issue, anti-abortion voters. These challengers are Christian Americans who understand that such religious leaders are espousing a position of political expedience and definitely not an expression of God's will.

In April of 2018, I interviewed a devout Catholic I met while researching my book about refugee resettlement. She was a mother, a community activist; she had worked in special education for twenty-five years. She was and remains all about making heaven happen right here on earth. She is against abortion. But in the 2016 presidential election, she weighed her choices. She voted for Hillary Clinton. The reason? "Once you get out of the womb, she's the true pro-life candidate," she told me.

VandeHei expressed that same sentiment. NPR's Martin pressed VandeHei asking how anyone who is anti-abortion could vote for Biden. VandeHei made it clear that Not Our Faith messaging was not going to change the minds of many evangelicals and Catholics. But, she said, it might be just what's necessary to tip the scales for Christians who have their doubts about Donald Trump, who hear the *nilch'iyazhi*, that whisper-voice in the backs of their heads.

NPR's Martin, playing devil's advocate, said some Trump supporters who recognize that the president's lifestyle is the antithesis of a Christian life rationalize this contradiction by saying that God often uses flawed people to advance his work on earth.

VandeHei knew her Bible.

"Yep," she said, "they use David all the time. They use Cyrus all the time," referring to David, the flawed hero of the Bible, and Cyrus, the Persian king who did not believe in God but allowed Jews to rebuild their temple in Jerusalem.

"I think people are twisting scripture," she said, adding that "different scriptures and different chapters of the Bible have been used since the beginning of politics everywhere to justify all kinds of horrendous things."

Not Our Faith's home page describes Trump as being "one of the greatest purveyors of debauchery, greed and immorality. This has continued into his presidency, and it won't stop until we elect to replace him."

This PAC is a group that told Trump that at this group of the faithful were no longer willing to save him at the polls. They said: Not this time. Not our vote. Not our faith. And they became part of the coalition that put Joe Biden into office.

Meet another progressive Christian.

Pope Francis.

Look at the pope's 2018 "Gaudete et Exsultate," which basically means "Rejoice and Be Glad." The pontiff was clear in defending what he called the "innocent unborn," (although my Catholic teachers taught us that we were all born with original sin, it's like a native app with us humans, y'know?) But he did not confine his pro-life stance to the unborn. He said "Equally sacred are the lives of the pure, those already born," he wrote.

Right. To be pro-life is to support an entire package. A package that takes care of us after birth every step of the way, from the moment we are born until we die. And that means providing good health care, making sure everyone is well fed, well housed, well educated and has access to equal opportunity.

Pope Francis continued expanding the definition of being pro-life in a general audience in June 2020.

That's when he said, "We cannot tolerate or turn a blind eye to racism and exclusion in any form and yet claim to define the sacredness of every human life."

Then, the pope made this even clearer when, just before Halloween 2020, a notification popped up on my phone: "Pope Francis Calls for Civil Unions for Same-Sex Couples." I stopped what I was doing to read more. He had certainly been dropping broad hints for years. But this was pretty explicit. His rationale? Homosexuals, he said, "have a right to be a part of the family."

He called them "children of God" who "have a right to a family."

To my disappointment, the Vatican has since barred gay unions, but it did uphold welcoming and blessing gay people. It's not enough, of course, but this is the Catholic Church. Look how long it took to accept that the earth revolves around the sun. It is not exactly an agent of change.

Nonetheless, Pope Francis's pro-life package is pretty damn clear. To be pro-life means taking care of people, both the born and unborn, fighting racism, including LGBTQ in the community. Wholeheartedly.

If you're not doing that, you can't call yourself pro-life. You're merely anti-abortion. There's a difference. The Republican Party is not pro-life. It's just anti-abortion.

The Republican Party has callously played the abortion card to win elections — and then failed to take care of the already born. Crucially, that includes pregnant women and young children.

The states pushing for the most restrictions on abortion tend to have the nation's highest infant mortality rates: Georgia, Ohio, Missouri, Louisiana, Alabama and Mississippi.[7] Four of these states refused to expand Medicaid under the Affordable Care Act. That expansion would have provided health care coverage for a lot of pregnant mothers. Healthy mothers have healthy babies. It's very, very simple. But the anti-abortion movement ignores that.

So, you're an unborn baby. Your mom gives birth to you. But she doesn't get adequate health care. So you, little unborn baby, you die. But at least you weren't aborted. Or so the anti-abortion stance seems to me.

I am not calling for more abortions. I am calling for saving babies by investing in policies that help babies be born and *live.*

And it's not just the babies who are dying. More and more pregnant women in America are dying.

The pregnancy mortality rate in America has more than doubled in the last thirty years. It has gone from 7.2 deaths per 100,000 live births in 1987 to 16.9 deaths per 100,000 live births in 2016.

If you're a Black woman, your chances of dying are way higher. That's right, Republican Party. Don't just disenfranchise people of color. Let women of color die in childbirth. That way they can't vote and they can't raise kids who can vote.

The death rate per 100,000 live births in 2016 was 42.4 for Black, non-Hispanic women; 30.4 for Native American women. For white, non-Hispanic women, the death rate was 13 per 100,000 live births. For all of these groups, the death rate was still higher than the national average of 7.2 in 1987.

The fact that the death rate for Black women is more than three times that of white women is a stunningly horrible statistic. It is unacceptable. It is also unacceptable that women are dying at higher rates on average than in the recent past.

Infant mortality transcends race. It is also about geography. Overall, infant mortality is lowest in cities and highest in rural areas — and rural America is increasingly Republican.

Here are a few more stats about the problem with making abortion the single issue on which you base your pro-life vote. Once babies are born in the United States, a lot of them don't get enough to eat.

Approximately one in five American children go hungry at some point in every year. One in seven worry about their next meal. In addition, America is a land of food deserts, both urban and rural. The US Department of Agriculture defines a food desert as urban areas with no market with fresh and nutritious food within one mile of one's home. In rural America, it's defined as living ten miles or more from such a market. It also includes not living near a food pantry or food-sharing program.

An estimated 23 million Americans live in a food desert. That's 23 million people without access to good nutrition. That's also a major reason we have a higher obesity rate and lower life expectancy than other Organization for Economic Cooperation and Development (OECD) countries.

Next up: Let's look at health insurance. Democrats created the Affordable Care Act, insured more Americans than ever before and mandated coverage of preexisting conditions. Republicans have devoted themselves to destroying that protection while offering no alternatives. Er, and they call themselves pro-life? Well sure, if you're going to lie, lie big.

Now there are exceptions to this, devout people of faith who help the poor and fight for voter rights and oppose racism. The rest of us just didn't see them because we bought into the right's rebranding of religion.

I've found that open-minded people of faith are everywhere once you start looking for them. Meanwhile, I've also found that there *are* progressive people of faith. As I hope is already clear, you don't have to be secular to be progressive. In fact, there are some Christians who are downright leftist!!

The Christian Left (www.TheChristianLeft.org) is a group for those who are Christian and liberal, and it shows that these are not mutually exclusive terms. I joined a similarly named group on Facebook. It's called: The Christian Left: Trinitarian Christianity & the Economic Left. The group's main credo: love. As in loving your neighbor, loving your enemy (I am definitely wrestling with that one) and recognizing that love is the heart of Christianity. The group asks you three questions: 1) Do you affirm the Nicene Creed? 2) Do you identify as a leftist and affirm egalitarianism, economic justice, social justice and cooperative economics? and 3) Do you agree to participate with civility?

I said the Nicene Creed every Sunday at church growing up and basically it says you believe in one God and that God came down from heaven. I am not sure about the coming down from heaven part. So I messaged that to the group moderator while adding that I respect those who embrace it.

In response to another question, I also said that I had been Ridin' With Biden (meaning he was my choice for the Democratic nominee early on).

My doubts about the Nicene Creed were not a problem. But my early embrace of Joe Biden was! Upon learning that, the group moderator wanted to make sure I was not going to promote centrism, centrist politicians or conservative or right-wing positions.

Oh. My. God. I love religious types who are to the left of me!

I promised to respect both the Nicene Creed and the fact that the group is to the left of me. "What I like," I wrote to the moderator, "is the way you are melding faith and leftist ideals. Do you know how refreshing and rare that is?"

The moderator got that, then said, "If things were the way they should be, the melding of Christian faith and leftist ideals would be old and common."

I hang out on the website just because it makes me so happy to see believers embrace the same attitudes and policy issues I do. Because I do rather like the picture that Charlie Seitz conjured of Jesus, as discussed in chapter 8. He and his wife Rebeca were trying to determine if there were a place in Christianity for those who did not take the Bible literally. So Charlie researched the historical Jesus and realized that the historical Jesus was a real rabble-rouser. The kind who would fit right into that Facebook group.

I hope that this is helping you see a different kind of Christian, not some insufferable, unctuous fake, but instead, someone who acts, who cares about issues like keeping kids healthy, giving them clean air to breath.

Now, let me tell you a bit more about us secular types. Some sociologists and theologians see us as a religious group, those who are unaffiliated. Defining us as a religious group makes the unaffiliated the fastest growing religious group in the nation. When asked for our religious affiliation, we check the box that says "none." Thus, our name: the nones. On dating apps, a lot of us say we're "spiritual." But we don't go to services or do so rarely. Some of us are totally secular. Some of us believe in God and consider ourselves religious. We just don't belong to a church or other formal religious institution.

A lot of us believe in God or a universal spirit, according to Pew Research, which does continual studies on American attitudes and beliefs about religion. A big chunk — 42 percent — say they are neither religious nor spiritual. But more of us describe ourselves as religious (18 percent) or as spiritual but not religious (37 percent). A lot of us have a pretty jaded view of affiliated religious groups. We say that religious organizations are too concerned about money and power, too focused on rules and too involved in politics.[8] We are also pretty skeptical about religious organizations' ability to solve social problems. I am with that group — because the Christian right is basically creating more social problems.

But I know progressive churches can be part of the solution. Some of my most effective work as an activist has been enabled by churches. When I was trying to help refugees. Rutgers Presbyterian Church gave me the opportunity to help resettle two refugee families from Syria. When I went to the Women's March on Washington in January 2017, I went on one of three buses that Rutgers booked. And when those buses joined the sea of buses parked at the RFK Stadium parking lot, a lot of them were from churches.

My then-synagogue, B'nai Jeshurun, gave me the opportunity to help set up the synagogue's refugee resettlement committee. Rutgers and B'nai Jeshurun are now partners on a variety of social justice issues.

When Empire State Indivisible, the political activist group in New York that I belong to, needed a place to meet, we met in churches. When we wrote Get Out the Vote (GOTV) postcards, we used a room at Fourth Universalist Society, a church on Manhattan's Upper West Side. Most of us were not members of these congregations. They just opened their doors to us. The political issues we were working on — voter rights, equal housing, welcoming refugees and immigrants — were also causes that churches and synagogues have long supported.

After all, Jesus was a Jew who was all about taking care of the "other."

Just days before the November 2020 election, the National Council of Churches (NCC) issued a press statement in which it decried racism and declared its support and admiration for peaceful protestors. It stated that this nation cannot move forward if it allows racism and white supremacy to continue to wreak havoc in our society. And it called racism a "sin that has plagued this nation since its inception."

It called on the federal government to lead a coordinated strategy to fight this pandemic. It said that wearing facemasks, observing physical distancing and avoiding crowds were "reasonable acts of service for Christians to make sure we are doing our part to protect the lives of the most vulnerable among us." The statement said the nation stood at an abyss, and we have a choice. To fall into it — or to step back from the brink. "Can we stand united and love our neighbors? Especially those who are not just like us?" Or, it went on to ask,

'Will we allow fear, divisions and hatred of others to rule the day?"

Why is the national council important? Because the NCC includes thirty-eight member groups accounting for more than forty million individuals in 100,000 congregations from Protestant (including evangelical), Anglican, Orthodox, historic African American and Living Peace traditions. Member denominations commit to advocating God's love and the promise of unity. NCC works with secular and interfaith groups to advance a shared agenda of peace, progress and positive change. That's a lot of people. They're just not as loud as evangelicals on their own.

Two important takeaways from this: First, 100,000 congregations is a lot of churches. Second, these are churches ready and willing to work not just with other faiths, but with the secular as well. They are up and running already.

So, my secular, agnostic and atheist friends, what are you waiting for?

Go find a damn church with a rainbow flag or a BLM banner and get to work!

---

[1] MATTHEWS, Mary Beth. "The History of Black Evangelicals and American Politics." *Black Perspectives."* March 30, 2017. https://www.aaihs.org/the-history-of-black-evangelicals-and-american-politics/

[2] Daniels III, David D. *The Conversation.* October 30, 2020. https://theconversation.com/the-black-church-has-been-getting-souls-to-the-polls-for-more-than-60-years-145996

[3] "Archbishop Clarifies Trump Rally." Archdiocese of Milwaukee *News Detail.* March 11, 2020. https://www.archmil.org/News-2.0/Archbishop-Clarifies-Trump-Rally.htm

⁴ Wootson, Cleve W. "Rev. William Barber builds a moral movement. *The Washington Post.* June 29, 2017. https://www.washingtonpost.com/news/acts-of-faith/wp/2017/06/29/woe-unto-those-who-legislate-evil-rev-william-barber-builds-a-moral-movement/

⁵ Smith, Samuel. Christians speak out as migrant children are detained without soap, hygiene needs." *The Christian Post.* June 25, 2019. https://www.christianpost.com/news/christians-speak-out-as-migrant-children-are-detained-without-soap-hygiene-needs.html\

⁶ Carey, Galen. "Responding to the Current Refugee Crisis." National Association of Evangelicals. February 2, 2017. https://www.nae.net/responding-current-refugee-crisis/

⁷ Edwards, Erika. "States pushing abortion bans have higher infant mortality rates." *NBC News.* May 24, 2019. https://www.nbcnews.com/health/womens-health/states-pushing-abortion-bans-have-higher-infant-mortality-rates-n1008481

⁸ "Religion and the Unaffiliated, 'Nones' on the Rise." Pew Research Center. October 9, 2012. https://www.pewforum.org/2012/10/09/nones-on-the-rise-religion/

11

WORKING THE MARGINS WITH JESUS

Here's why I'm telling you to find a church. Not to join it. Not to sing praises of Jesus there — unless you want to. But to work with the people in that church to protect our freedom.

Get this: Voters of faith helped put Joe Biden over the top.[1]

In the months before the 2020 election, some polls and surveys showed that Trump's support among Catholics and white evangelicals was slipping. The president's campaign staff stoutly denied it.

From 47 percent to 50 percent of Catholic voters supported Trump in 2020. That was only a little less than he got in 2016, but enough to cost him some crucial rust belt states. Ditto white evangelicals. A lot voted for him in 2020 — 76 percent to 78 percent of them. In 2016, 81 percent of white evangelicals voted for Trump.[1] That slippage among both groups was just enough to deliver states like Georgia[2], Pennsylvania and Wisconsin to Biden. Remember the Not Our Faith bipartisan super PAC that ran pro-Biden ads targeting Christian voters? It knew those kinds of doubters were out there and persuadable. Now you know it, too.

Drill down to the state level and here's more encouraging news. Biden won 29 percent of the white evangelical vote in Michigan. Clinton got 14 percent in 2016. He more than doubled that!

In Georgia, Biden won 14 percent compared to Clinton's 5 percent in 2016. In short, he tripled that vote!

Catholics and white evangelicals who swung for Biden aren't the only ones who put Biden over the top. But, they hold a lesson for us. And that is there are members on the margins of a lot of groups who look like they'll vote for the Republican Party of today, but who actually will vote Democratic.

Here are a few more of them.

The suburbs helped Biden win, too. They shifted from majority Republican in 2016 to majority Democrat in 2020.[2] Take Oconomowoc, Wisconsin. It's a pretty lakeside town in traditionally Waukesha County, which is part of what's now called the WOW counties—the traditionally Republican strongholds Waukesha, Ozaukee and Washington counties that ring Milwaukee. Biden won 37,000 more votes there than Hillary Clinton did in 2016. Trump upped his votes, too, by 29,000. Waukesha remains Republican. But it's a little less Republican than it was.[3] Remember that!

The Black vote was a huge help in putting Biden over the top, with nine out of 10 Black voters in his camp. Black voters saved the day.[4]

Young voters, particularly young voters of color, went strongly for Biden.[5] Whites still went Republican — but not to the same degree in 2020 as in 2016.[6]

The only Republican stronghold where Biden didn't gain much was among rural voters. We really have to work at winning over these voters, and here's why. Although rural voters are shrinking in number, they have a disproportionate amount of power. They also are angry. They feel left behind and with good reason. The Rural Democracy Initiative, which invests in civic and political change in rural areas, reports that regressive interests have invested heavily in rural America just as progressive leadership and funding withdrew,

Rural hospitals are closing or struggling. Many rural Americans survive only by working piecemeal jobs. Farming is under siege. Wisconsin's Monroe County — where my family has lived for five generations, sometimes supported by farming — and neighboring Vernon County, led the nation in farm bankruptcies in 2019.

Rural Americans feel left out. And yes, I know, blue states subsidize red states with their tax dollars but red state residents are still suffering. Why are they suffering? Because they're voting for Republicans. Why are they voting for Republicans? Because Republicans do a better job of marketing. Plus, right-wing media, from Fox News to the conservative Sinclair Broadcast Group, dominate the airwaves.

Rural voters illustrate the Democratic Party's branding problem. They also illustrate opportunity. Remember, there's a big minority of Democrats in those areas already. A lot of them lie low. They are scared. When I called Monroe County Democrats during the 2020 presidential campaign to make sure they knew their voting options, two or three of them wanted to make sure that I was really a Democrat and not some Trumper trying to find Democrats to threaten. Fortunately for me, I could reassure them.

"I'm Jim and Barbara Rice's daughter," I'd say. "Remember the sand mine fight? That was my mother and me," referring to a 2012 campaign in the county to try to stop frac sand mines from moving into townships in our county that had little or no zoning. I could go through a long list of campaigns designed to protect or improve the community that my mother, father or other relatives had been part of. Obviously, we've got a lot of work to do in rural America. But for every person who wanted to vet me, there were two who wanted yard signs — including in neighborhoods with a lot of active and retired military families.

But our opportunity in rural America lies not just with the Democrats who are already there and whom we want to reassure and empower. Obama's data guru Dan Wagner, now CEO of Civis Analytics, has pointed out that states that went solidly for Trump, states like Florida, Montana and South Dakota, also voted yes on progressive initiatives like a substantially higher minimum wage and legalized weed.

Democrats stand for so many policies that Americans support — better pay, better jobs, clean air, water and soil. Democrats are also for better health care. And Republicans are really vulnerable when it comes to health care. Republicans thought they were dancing on the grave of the Affordable Care Act in 2017. And then they went home for the February 2017 Congressional recess. They found themselves bombarded by furious constituents. Trump's rating plummeted.

The ACA survived. Remember that.

The 2020 election results show where opportunity lies for Democrats in rural areas. Biden tended to win rural counties where there are more non-white minorities. Rural counties that Biden won in the South were facing tougher economic times. Conversely, Biden won more prosperous rural counties in the Northeast. In the West, Biden did much better in rural counties where a lot of residents work in the tourism industry.

Now, back to branding. Republicans have defined the Democrats as godless, baby-killing socialists who support big government that will take away our freedoms. And we Democrats allowed that! A lot of us (not me) even use the deceptive term the abortion opponents coined for themselves, pro-life! I don't. But the media and most progressives do.

We are actually the party of life but we have lost control of our brand.

The Democratic Party is the party of the working class, but it is all too easily seen as the fancy-pants party. That's a diversion tactic that the Republicans have used to hide the fact that the Republican Party is still the party of big business. It's the party that takes care of the already rich. Now, the rich are a minority. This party of the rich — which is mostly white — has been working for decades to split us Democrats (something we make very easy for them to do because we are natural squabblers) while they are in lockstep (authoritarianism is quite efficient). Trump is the culmination of this. He truly was the man for the moment. His angry populist message resonated with voters who felt forgotten by big-city liberals, whom they believe paid more attention to cities. So, a lot of rural voters who are not rich and powerful keep voting for the party of the rich and powerful.

All of this said, there are a lot of issues with which we can grow our margins. We have an advantage with LGBTQ rights. The nation has flipped on this in the past twenty-five years. This is particularly true among young voters, included young evangelicals. As usual, those clever and shameless Republicans have found a fear tactic — they lie and say trans kids will threaten straight kids in the locker room and in the fight for sports scholarships (this seems to be having more success in the South). Targeting vulnerable kids. Disgusting.

Climate change is another issue in which Democrats have an advantage. Pew Research reported in May 2021 that majorities of Americans say the Federal government is not doing enough to fight climate change. This is especially true among Gen Zers (the youngest voters, born between 1997 and 2012) and Millennials ((born between 1981 and 1996).[7]

I think law enforcement is another place of opportunity for Democrats. Republicans call themselves the party of law and order, but they sent thousands of armed insurrectionists to attack police protecting our nation's Capitol, and then stood in the way of investigating that attack on the police. Republican Congressmen are telling the men and women in blue who defended not just the Capitol but the lives of members of Congress that nothing happened that day. We have to exploit that. We have to put billboards across the nation showing insurrectionists beating Capitol police next to photos of Republican members of Congress who lie and say it never happened, or that it wasn't that bad. These police men and women risked their lives to save the lives of these members of Congress who are so power mad and ungrateful that they are denying that the attack on the Capitol and on *them, members of Congress themselves,* happened!

But it's not just the police in our nation's capital who are suffering. Hate-mongering groups create headaches and work for police departments across the country.

Republicans can combat that by linking Defund the Police movements with Joe Biden. This is a lie. He rejected calls to defund police and promised to *double* funding for community policing. We have to shout from the rooftops that Joe Biden is actually *re-funding* police. In July 2021, the White House encouraged state and local governments to use money from the $350 billion American Rescue Plan, the official name of the Covid relief bill, to hire more police and train more police.[8]

In addition, we have to publicize the fact that Democrats have put money in people's pockets with the latest Covid relief bill and the new child tax credit, which pays most parents $250 or $300 a month *per kid,* the amount determined by the age of each child. I say, let's put billboards across the country with the $250/$300 per month figures and a photo of the local member of Congress. If it's a Republican, shame that Republican for voting against the interests of his or her constituents. If it's a

Democrat, praise him or her for voting to improve the lives of constituents.

It's time for Democrats to take charge of language and reframe the conversation. We want to go easy on using party labels. Here is why. Political affiliation is part of our identity. It's in our bones. We Democrats have to talk less about Republican and Democratic and talk more about issues. Those issues include affordable health care, infrastructure, good jobs, clean air, equal rights for all and protecting our right to vote. We need to showcase the integrity of our voting system by talking about the honest, hardworking municipal and county clerks across the country who are committed to fair and honest elections. The Republican Big Lie about the 2020 presidential election says these clerks failed at their jobs. But they actually protected our votes. City, town and county clerks run elections in this country. They are unsung heroes and they have long been the guardians of our democracy.

We have to keep the common ground with the disparate groups that swung just enough to put Joe Biden and Kamala Harris over the top. We've got to keep these voters energized. They have to feel empowered. They *should* feel empowered! Because in November 2020, they turned out in huge numbers, despite a global pandemic, long lines and lies designed to keep those voters home. Those efforts to block our freedom to vote failed thanks to those determined and brave voters.

A majority of American voters turned out and elected Joe Biden. And what has President Biden done since they put him in office? He put money in their pocketbooks so they could pay their bills. He vaccinated Americans who wanted to protect themselves from the pandemic. And when the Delta variant spread, it was hardest on the unvaccinated, making them far sicker than the unvaccinated and killing some of them. Joe Biden was able to save lives with his vaccination campaign. He could not have done this without the voters backing him for president.

Biden's supporters were voters of all faiths and of no faith, voters of all colors, rural voters, suburban voters, city voters. We activists have to keep working. Who are these activists? You, me, anyone. Anyone who wrote a postcard or called their representatives in Congress, their state legislatures or city hall. Anyone who marched for Black Lives Matter demonstrations in Sparta, Wisconsin, and small towns and big cities across this nation. We activists have to keep ourselves and all of those voters who voted for Joe Biden energized and help them spread a message.

Here is the message. We are fighting a frightened minority that has conquered the Republican Party. This minority can only win by lying and by spreading fear. Members of this minority are doing that to distract us from the fact that they're a racist party working to help the already rich, damn the rest of the nation. Not all Republicans are racist — far from it. But the forces that run the Republican Party of today are trying to take the vote away from Blacks, Native Americans and other people of color. Why are they racist? Because you can't win on fear unless you can create an us and a them. (Credit for that last observation goes to Anat Shenker Osorio, a strategic communications consultant whom I've listened to a few times on Pod Save America. I follow her religiously on Twitter on @anatosaurus).

This frightened minority's tactics: fear and division. This minority has been with us since the birth of our country, and it is a racist bunch. These folks fire up fear so that people won't notice what they are really doing. What they are really doing is making the rich richer and keeping the rest of us poorer.

That astute political observer and devout Catholic Caroline Heileman, the mother of one of my high school classmates in Sparta, Wisconsin, understood that long ago, when she told one of her daughters who asked about politics.: "Republicans want to make the rich richer and the poor poorer." Caroline Heileman grew up on a farm up on the Ridge (that same Ridge where my high school boyfriend and I used to park and make out), married a small businessman who ran a local gas station and raised seven kids. She considered abortion murder, but the Republicans couldn't fool her. When you get up in arms about the anti-abortion movement, remember Caroline Heileman, who died in 1996. She didn't always vote for Democrats. But sometimes she did. We have to be sure that we can give voters like her a reason to vote for the true party of life.

Now, back to the way this frightened minority is operating today. It gives the rich lots of tax breaks, but offers nothing like that for the rest of us. Working people pay a higher percentage of the dollars they sweated for in taxes than the rich. The rich pay their smaller overall tax rates on money that they, for the most part, did *not* sweat for. And then this minority talks about our "big-spending government." This is a fear tactic that the party of the rich uses to scare everyday taxpayers, those of us who pay a far bigger percentage of our income on taxes than the rich. It's a lie designed to make every day Americans afraid that the government is going to raise our taxes even more. The government that does that is a Republican controlled government.

Notice I am talking about a racist minority, I am not calling them Republicans. (Again, I thank Anat Shenker Osorio although there are plenty of other smart people out there who recognize this.) Right now, this racist minority has made its home with the Republican Party. Republicans are not necessarily racist, but the party they support is pushing racist policies. In the past, racism had a home with the Democratic Party. Today, the Democratic Party is the party of freedom, the party that protects everyone's right to vote, the party for affordable health care for all, the party for equal opportunity for all.

We're the party of black, white and brown. We're from cities, small towns and farm country. We're in the North, the West, the East and the South (thank you again, Georgia!).

We want to remind these voters of what they did in 2020 and tell them they can do it again in 2022 and in 2024.

Now I know you're saying, "*Oh, Kate, Trump this, Republicans that, etc., etc.*"

This is exactly what the racist minority currently possessing the Republican Party wants you to think, that its tactics will be successful — when it *has been losing!* This losing minority wants you to think that its victory is inevitable.

Freedom in this country has a history of squeaking through by the skin of its teeth. In 1787, the Confederation Congress approved the Northwest Ordinance, which included what would become Illinois, Indiana, Michigan, Ohio and Wisconsin. In creating this territory and laying the path for statehoods, this Congress also banned slavery in the territory. It was the first free zone in the United States. It was imperfect; slave owners could chase and capture runaway slaves in this territory.

Slavery's supporters did not give ground easily. In 1799, the Northwest Territorial Legislature voted to make Ohio a state. Judge Ephraim Cutler introduced a clause in that resolution making Ohio a free state. That resolution and the anti-slavery cause passed by a *single* vote. In his book, *The Pioneers,* author David McCullough describes that vote. Judge Cutler was too sick to walk and had to be carried on a litter in order to cast that deciding vote. One vote.

Can you imagine how different our history would have been if not for Judge Cutler? Here was a man who wrestled with self-doubt about himself. He struggled to support his family. He would bury two of his children on the wilderness trail they traveled when he moved his family west from New England to Ohio. And then, after they arrived in Ohio, his wife died. Being

Ephraim Cutler was *hard*. What if he had not written that clause into the statehood document? What if he had thought that slavery was inevitable and stayed in his sickbed? What if he had given up without even trying? What if he had said on the day of the vote, "Guys, I am puking my guts out, I can't come"? But Ephraim Cutler was not that kind of guy. He was a guy who faced long odds, defeat and crippling grief and kept trying. He was my kind of guy.

I can hear you saying already, *"Oh, Kate, you Pollyanna, haven't you read the news?"*

My response: Take what you read in the news with a grain of salt. And I am not talking Fox or Sinclair, I am talking *The New York Times, Wall Street Journal,* CNN, all of them!

They do a lot of good reporting but they are so committed to being "unbiased" that they give equal play to progressives fighting for our voting rights and to liars propagating the big Republican lie *although they know it is a lie!* Look at a reporter who interviews a progressive legislator pushing for, say, a bill to fight climate change. The reporter then has to interview an opponent of the bill, who is a climate change denier. This is like interviewing someone who has circumnavigated the earth proving it is round and then interviewing some nut who still makes a case that the earth is flat. This is not to present a well-rounded story. This is to prove that the reporter is "unbiased." It's not about truth.

The media have finally started to put the adjective "false" in front of those lies. But this is a relatively new development. And, frankly, pretty weak. I'm glad they're doing it, but they've got to start giving context and using good judgment about whom they quote. Is this person saying one word of truth? If it is one giant lie, let Fox cover it.

The media also jump from one story to another. News is, well, what's new. Just because it's new doesn't make it important.

But the media do not seem to get that, or at least, they don't act on it. The child tax credit, especially if it is made permanent, could change the economics for this country for the better in a way we haven't seen since FDR's New Deal. But is it getting that kind of coverage?

No.

Now, there is a lot going on, I will give you that. But using this thing called judgment is a way to deal with that.

Here's another thing to remember as you read stories that make you want to crawl back into bed or reach for a very large bottle of something alcoholic. Dramatic rhetoric is part of the legislative process. Wrangling over big bills and changing them is part of the legislative process. There's a lot of brinkmanship. The inside-the-beltway press should know this. But this doesn't seem so when the press declares a big bill is on the ropes or doomed. Part of it is the race for clicks — who is going to click on a story that says things are moving along as usual in Washington? But an apocalyptic headline about an infrastructure bill? That's something we'll click on.

So, take what you read with a grain of salt. Avoid doom scrolling. Try not to get too caught up in the twittersphere.

In scary times like these, it's important to watch for the victories and to celebrate them. The child tax credit program that I already mentioned is one of those. Yes, there have been some stories that did recognize the importance of this legislation, which produced the first checks to most parents in America in July 2021.

One of those stories was in *The Washington Post*, which described it as "the biggest anti-poverty program undertaken by the federal government in more than half a century." The majority of American parents are getting these checks. And this program is massively popular. On the July 19, 2021, Pod Save America podcast, the show's hosts talked about focus groups in which Trump voters said the program would make them rethink their votes in upcoming election. It would bring fundamental change to this country. But we've got to be relentless in talking about it, focusing on it and running on it! It's important for you to do this because this is a way to fight the far right minority.

Stop fretting about Trump running again in 2024. He might run! If he doesn't, Republicans will find someone very like him to run. But there's no return in worrying about it. To do so means you are doing exactly what the far right wants you to do: obsessing about what they are doing to take away our freedoms instead of fighting for our right to vote. The right loves stories about the dire threat it presents because it hopes that such stories will paralyze us and discourage us.

It's easy to get depressed. Covid kept us from loved ones and added to our workloads (just talk to any mother with kids still at home) and intensified our worries. So make time to play. Have friends for dinner, go for a walk, start a hobby, binge on *Bridgerton*, listen to comic podcasts. Our brains need entertainment and stories that take us out of our own (if you want to know more about this, please read Lisa Feldman Barrett's *The Secret Life of the Brain: How Emotions Are Made* or watch her TED Talk. She's a professor at Northeastern University whose research has revolutionized psychology and neuroscience.)

Here's what's important.

We've got a window of opportunity here. There is recent history of people from across the political spectrum working together on issues that they agree on. Proof of this: refugee resettlement. This issue, so polarizing in the headlines, is unifying on the ground. Churches, including conservative churches in red states, have long worked to help refugees. Churches can be social justice machines; they can attract their secular neighbors. Although these volunteers working together to help refugees might have voted for different candidates and may have opposing views on abortion and LGBTQ rights, they do agree about refugee resettlement. And they work shoulder to shoulder with people from across the political spectrum to help those refugees.

Arkansas, Idaho, Iowa, Kentucky, North Carolina, Texas and Utah that are home to robust refugee resettlement programs. These groups have cosponsored refugee families when they arrived here. Some even went to Washington, DC, to lobby their conservative representatives to pressure the Trump Administration to raise the numbers of refugees allowed to enter the country (pre-Covid). Evangelical and other conservative leaders have testified before Congress, praising our nation's refugee program. Religious leaders have taken out full-page ads in places like the *New York Times* to spread the word of their support for refugees.

There are other indicators that we can find minds open to challenging the authoritarian tenets of the Christianity they were raised in. That sets the stage for challenging a Republican Party that has sold its soul to Christian nationalism.

You can find these indicators on *The New York Times* Best Seller list. These are authors, many raised on absolute faith, who have listened to that tiny voice, Sylvia Clahchischilli's *nilch'iyazhi*, in their heads pushing them to question their beliefs.

Many are part of a vanguard of progressive Christian women who challenged the beliefs they were taught. They include Nadia Bolz-Weber, Glennon Doyle, Jen Hatmaker and Barbara Brown Taylor and the late Rachel Held Evans. All are bestselling authors and women of faith who challenge the precepts of the religious right. And they have an audience.

Most of these authors come from a tradition that interprets the Bible literally. And they are writing books with titles like

Leaving Church, Interrupted: When Jesus Wrecks Your Comfortable Christianity and *Shameless: A Sexual Reformation.*

Evans, who died tragically young at thirty-seven in 2019, spent her teenage years in Dayton, Tennessee, site of the Scopes trial. She grew up in a tradition of interpreting the Bible literally. Her father taught at a Christian liberal arts college in Dayton. But she heard that whisper, that *nilch'iyazhi*, and allowed herself to doubt.

One of her books, *Faith Unraveled: How a Girl Who Knew All the Answers Learned to Ask Questions,* chronicles her own doubts about the Christianity in which she was raised. That book gave me an inside and frightening look at the beliefs among conservative Christians. And she tackled them, head on. These are religious insiders who are asking the kinds of questions that can give some people permission to listen to the doubts about conservative Christian teaching that they have been trying to ignore.

Not surprisingly, all of these authors have participated in the Wild Goose Festival. It's not just women challenging Christian nationalism and authoritarianism. There are men, too. An Amazon best-selling author endorsed by these authors is Brian D. McLaren, who has written several hits, the latest being *Faith After Doubt.* He, too, is allied with the Wild Goose Festival. He has accused the religious right of grooming its church members to follow authoritarian leaders.

"Something is deeply, dangerously wrong with white Christianity in America," he said in a Zoom presentation he made to the Wild Goose community that I watched just before President Biden's Inauguration.

McLaren was raised a liberal Protestant,[6] but was drawn to the evangelical sense of a personal relationship to Jesus. But, as a pro-choice Democrat and supporter of the rights of the LGBTQ community, he kept his distance.

These authors don't just talk religion in their writing, they take their beliefs into the world we inhabit today. Doyle's memoir, *Untamed*, covers a lot of territory. But in it she uses misogyny and religious oppression as springboards for a discussion of how those two evils feed racism.

Authoritarian religion and authoritarian regimes are not two separate topics. They are the same. As McLaren said in his Zoom talk, religious leaders who encourage blind trust in leaders quash critical thought and groom their followers for authoritarian governments.

Social media, conservative media outlets and Christian publishing companies bring massive scale to this.

The result, the religious right has become an aggregator of followers groomed for authoritarianism. By effectively grooming their adherents to accept despots, conservative Christian leaders make them easy marks for the likes of Trump and his ilk. Fortunately, there has been a backlash against him.

A number of religious leaders are issuing their own mea culpas.

In a fiery editorial the day after the January 6 assault on the U.S. Capitol, *The Catholic Reporter* first justifiably condemned the president and his minions in the House and Senate whose support of the president and his lies helped fan the flames of the domestic attack. But then, it looked right at the Catholic Church, and here is what it said about the church's complicity. "Catholic apologists for Trump have blood on their hands."

It's a searing indictment. Here's an excerpt.

"This is the culmination of what this presidency has been about from the beginning — and some Catholics have remained silent, or worse, cheered it along, including some bishops, priests, a few sisters, right-wing Catholic media and too many people in the pro-life movement. [9]

"We're talking to you CatholicVote.org, Attorney General

William Barr and other Catholics in the Trump administration, Amy Coney Barrett, Cardinal Timothy Dolan, Bill Donohue of the Catholic League, rogue pro-lifer Abby Johnson. Sadly, the list goes on."

There have always been evangelical opponents to the melding of the religious right with extreme right wingers. After the January 6 attack on the Capitol, Ed Stetzer, executive director of the Billy Graham Center at Wheaton College, an evangelical college in Illinois, wrote in an editorial in *USA Today* that Trump "has burned down the Republican Party, emboldened white supremacists, mainstreamed conspiracy theorists and more."

And then he turned on his fellow evangelicals.

"Tempted by power and trapped within a culture war theology, too many evangelicals tied their fate to a man who embodied neither their faith nor their vision of political character."[10]

Hundreds of faculty and staff at Wheaton signed a statement condemning the attack on the Capitol. The first sentence read:

"The January 6 attack on the Capitol was characterized not only by vicious lies, deplorable violence, white supremacy, white nationalism and wicked leadership — especially by President Trump — but also by idolatrous and blasphemous abuses of Christian symbols."[11]

A shameful number of evangelical leaders have supported Trump and his lies. And a shameful number will continue to do so.

Every time you hear people linking God with their support of Trump, it is important to remember that somewhere nearby are those who doubts such rhetoric, who are open to working with people who are not part of their religion, but who are on the same side I'm on when it comes to big issues like health care, voter suppression, racism and climate change.

Now a lot of us nones, us unaffiliated, are believers. I believe in God — but I don't believe that God works through only one religious institution. Some of us believe in the universe, which I think can be another word for God.

A lot of us believe in justice. Justice is as fundamental to this world as gravity. It's just more ephemeral (I fulfilled my science requirement with a course called Physics for Poets, so you can challenge me on this one, no problem). But justice is there, and it might just be another name for *nilch'iyazhi*, that quiet little voice tapping away at the back of our skulls, gently, but persistently, telling us that something is happening that is not right.

Now how to put all this into practice? There are a few things to do. Look for your local chapter of Indivisible, a national network of grassroots organizing born in the dark days of November 2016 after the election. No matter what your schedule or your location, there is something you can do. This is a group that works from the ground up. Its goal: to make our elected officials accountable to the people. It works on campaigns on local, state and national levels. It works with existing groups. It works to elect officials and then it works to tell those elected officials what we, their constituents, want them to do for us. So this can be as easy as calling your representatives at city hall, the state legislature and Congress to tell them what you want them to vote for. Unless you tell them, they won't know what you, their constituents, their bosses, want. If you've got the time, it can mean working as a campaign volunteer. At whatever level you choose to participate, it'll be good for you — it will connect you with people with positive energy. Action is the antidote to anxiety.

Even if you're not from Wisconsin, sign up to make a small contribution to the Minocqua Brewing Company SuperPAC. This is a progressive brewing company in northern Wisconsin — yet another of the many places in our country that might look red but is really purple — fighting for small business. Its goal is to replace Ron Johnson in the U.S. Senate and Tom Tiffany in Congress, two right-wing politicians committed to lies. The Minocqua SuperPAC's fighting words will inspire you.

And, to repeat myself, look around for a church with a rainbow flag or a Black Lives Matter flag. It'll have a whole network of people for you to work with, and a lot of these church members will have the same views on some big issues as you do.

And remember, talk issues, not labels. Do you want to raise the minimum wage? Do you want better health care for everyone? Are you worried about our nation's crumbling infrastructure? Do you want to invest in rebuilding it? Do you want to rebuild with clean energy while producing new, good-paying jobs? Do you want clean water and clean air? Do you want to protect our right to vote? Do you want equal rights for all? Do you want more mothers to get good prenatal care so they can have healthy babies? Do you want the rich and corporations pay their fair share of taxes? Focus on that, not the Republican lies designed to distract us from the real issues.

Be aware of and ignore the media's obsession with Trump. The guy is not an aberration; he is the culmination of years of work by a Republican Party hijacked by the far right. The Republican Party got what it was looking for with Donald Trump. We're not fighting a man, we are fighting a minority that is trying to control the majority by attacking our election process. It has been doing so for decades.

Remember, you are not alone. There are *so many* of us out there! More of us than them! It's why this minority is running so scared.

So, I say, quit bitching about the Republicans who have sold their souls. Instead, stand strong with those of us who have hung onto them.

[1] Wear, Michael. "The Faithful Voters Who Helped Put Biden Over the Top. *The New York Times.* November 11, 2020. https://www.nytimes.com/2020/11/11/opinion/biden-evangelical-voters.html

[2] Florida, Richard; Patino, Marie; Dottle, Rachel. "How Suburbs Swung the 2020 Election." *Bloomberg City Lab.* November 17, 2020. https://www.bloomberg.com/graphics/2020-suburban-density-election/

[3] Drosher, Chris. "Let's Take a Deep Dive Into How the WOW Counties Voted." *Milwaukee Magazine.* November 5, 2020. https://www.milwaukeemag.com/lets-take-a-deep-dive-into-how-the-wow-counties-voted/

[4] Stafford, Kat; Morrison, Aaron; Kastanis, Angeliki. "'This is Proof': Biden's win reveals power of Black voters." AP News. November 9, 2020. https://apnews.com/article/election-2020-joe-biden-race-and-ethnicity-virus-outbreak-georgia-7a843bbce00713cfde6c3fdbc2e31eb7

[5] Nelson, Angela. "Young Voters Were Crucial to Biden's Win." *Tufts Now.* November 12, 2020. https://now.tufts.edu/articles/young-voters-were-crucial-biden-s-win

[6] Frey, William H. "Exit polls show both familiar and new voting blocs sealed Biden's win." *Brookings,* The Brookings Institute. November 12, 2020. https://www.brookings.edu/research/2020-exit-polls-show-a-scrambling-of-democrats-and-republicans-traditional-bases/

[7] Funk, Cary. "Key findings: How Americans' attitudes about climate change differ by generation, party and other factors." Pew Research Center. May 26, 2021. https://www.pewresearch.org/fact-tank/2021/05/26/key-findings-how-americans-attitudes-about-climate-change-differ-by-generation-party-and-other-factors/

[8] Klein, Betsy. "Biden Administration urging state and local governments to use Covid relief funding to address uptick in violent crime." CNN. July 12, 2021. https://www.cnn.com/2021/07/12/politics/biden-administration-crime-covid-relief-funding/index.html

[9] NCR Editorial Staff, "Catholics need to confess their complicity in the failed coup." *National Catholic Reporter,* January 7, 2021. https://www.ncronline.org/news/opinion/editorial-catholics-need-confess-their-complicity-failed-coupd

[10] Stetzer, Ed. "Evangelicals face a reckoning: Donald Trump and the future of our faith." USA Today. January 10, 2021. https://www.usatoday.com/story/opinion/2021/01/10/after-donald-trump-evangelical-christians-face-reckoning-column/6601393002/

[11] Redden, Elizabeth. "Wheaton College Faculty, Staff Condemn Capitol Attack." Inside Higher Ed. January 15, 2021. https://www.insidehighered.com/quicktakes/2021/01/15/wheaton-college-faculty-staff-condemn-capitol-attack

12
NOT THE END

I am ending this book but this story isn't over.

I am a totally secular political junkie whose politics were formed by the progressive Catholics who raised me. I grew up going to church. But, my religion didn't define me. Faith was part of my life, a part that irritated me when my parents made us kids go to Mass every Sunday. It was also a practice that I internalized despite my youthful protests. And there were parts of Catholicism that I considered beautiful. Not confession, of course, or hell, but there were aspects of beauty that I loved, in some of the Gospel readings during Mass, in some music and sometimes, in sermons or even in religion class.

I even loved some of the ritual. My attachment went so far that, at some young age, I wanted to be a nun. That probably happened after watching a really athletic nun on the playground skillfully kicking a soccer ball around with a bunch of kids, her skirt and veil flying in the wind.

That was a very brief flirtation.

Then, I discovered boys, and that took care of that. (It took boys a lot longer to discover me, though).

Here's how I became a none, one of those who checks the no-religious-affiliation box.

Catholicism and I ran into trouble over abortion. I grew up just as abortion took over the pulpit in Catholic churches. Priest after priest vilified abortion and told us to vote to end it. I felt the church had stepped over the line separating church and state and had become a political lobbying group. It had politicized God. Besides, calling abortion murder didn't make sense to me because whenever my aunts or a neighbor miscarried, none of them ever had a funeral for that fetus. And the reason they didn't was because the church didn't do funerals for fetuses. That showed me that even the Catholic Church did not consider a miscarriage the death of a human with a soul. So I was furious with the Catholic Church for two reasons. First, it was forcing its beliefs on people who chose not to be Catholic. Secondly, by not making a practice of funerals when women miscarried, it was, at best, inconsistent, at worst hypocritical. Finally, I considered it a step toward theocracy. I did not then and still do not want to live in a theocracy.

For a long time, I just sat there and steamed, figuring it was good for me to practice the self-discipline of keeping my mouth shut. But eventually, I decided keeping my mouth shut was bad for me. I wasn't going to stand up and start shouting from the pews, though I did fantasize about that sometimes. I once walked out, however.

So I started going to Episcopal churches. The liturgy was familiar and the incense smelled the same. But the first church I went to seemed as conservative as the Catholic Church I had just left. I remember coming home from Mass and putting my head in my then-boyfriend's lap.

"There's nowhere for me to go anymore," I moaned.

Although he was a totally nonobservant Jew at the time, he patted my head and offered sympathy.

Then, to my astonishment, when I mentioned I was going to get my prescription for birth control pills renewed, he said, "Actually, I was thinking about having kids."

After I picked myself up off the floor, I thought, *hmm!*

I immediately felt we should raise our kids as Jews. One of my dad's sisters and one of his brothers had married Jews. No big deal for my family. But those aunts and uncles did raise their kids as Catholics, and as a kid, I thought they should have raised one kid as a Jew and one as a Catholic. As an adult, I can see some of the impracticalities of that. Of course, the kid who was raised a Jew would love Christmas and the kid who was raised a Catholic would prefer the religion that actually blesses wine.

What I did not know at that time was that Judaism is matrilineal. That is, the mom has to be Jewish for the kids to be Jewish. Even once I learned that, I figured, "What the hell, I'll try it."

Frankly, I thought it fit with my view of myself as an outside-the-box type. Also, I'd fallen in love with the history of Israel as a kid when I was obsessed with World War I and World War II. That, of course, had meant learning about the Holocaust and establishment of the state of Israel.

As I learned about Judaism itself, I found a lot to like. You can be a Jew without having to believe in God. There is no Hebrew word for sin. There is a word meaning "to miss," as in, to miss the mark, but no word for sin. If you don't have sin, there's no need for hell. (When I found that out, Jewish guilt really baffled me — unless Jews felt guilty about not having to believe in hell). There's no need for baptism — so no limbo for those innocent babies who died before their parents could baptize them. Of course, there's no heaven either. In fact, Judaism is pretty fuzzy about an afterlife in general; it focuses on the here and now.

I liked the politics of the New York synagogue we joined. Its head rabbi had been active in the civil rights movement. Early on, the synagogue embraced gay marriage and officiated at same-sex marriages.

I admired my rabbis for many of the positions they took on racism, immigrants, refugees, LGBTQ rights, worker rights and more. Many fellow members of that synagogue were and are my partners in social justice and a lot of them inspire me. American Judaism isn't perfect; for example, I believe too many American Jews tippy-toed around the Israeli-Palestinian conflict for far too long and some still do.

The deal breaker for Judaism and me was that my ex-husband weaponized Judaism, making it yet another arrow to pull from his quiver of micro aggressions unleashed against me. He didn't know a helluva lot more about Judaism than I did because he had been raised by secular Jews who, he had told me, were bar mitzvah Jews. They went to synagogue until their kids completed their bar mitzvahs.

His parents had gotten divorced and both had then married WASPs (white Anglo-Saxon Protestants). They never went to synagogue. He never went to synagogue either. Until I converted.

In contrast, my parents had taken us to church every Sunday. We kids did not go docilely. Dad sometimes complained that taking us to church put him out of a state of grace. I cannot help wondering at the timing of my mother's switch from Episcopalian to Catholic. She did not convert until we all were out of the house. I think that's suspicious, don't you?

Still, I grew up with a religion in my life. When I left Catholicism, I tried to find a religion that didn't make me angry. That was happening just as my boyfriend and I were planning marriage and kids. I think my search turned us both into Jews, me by conversion, him by embracing the religion that he'd been born into.

Judaism is not a dogmatic religion. At least, not in my experience. In fact, Jews have — with centuries of written commentary — institutionalized debating what the Bible really means. That commentary is called the Midrash, or 'Drash, for short, just for fun. Commentaries focus on specific passages of the Bible, and there are commentaries on commentaries, also going back centuries. Literal interpretation of the Bible? Not possible.

But my husband was a born-again Jew and seemed to me to be as dogmatic as any born-again Christian I'd encountered. I'd be absorbed in the beauty of the music and the service, and he'd poke me for not following along in the prayer book. I was learning a new religion, new prayers, even a new language. (I was as bad at Hebrew as I was at Latin.) People praised me for how well I said the *kiddush*, the blessing of the wine (clearly, this was a natural for a party girl like me), but my husband pooh-poohed my achievement by saying it was a really easy prayer. When I went to the *bima* (the Hebrew word for altar) to do the Amidah — a series of blessings in which congregants join the rabbis at the altar to sing the blessings — he told me I wasn't practicing enough and should work harder at singing the prayer. And he was critical of my debut at the *bima*.

I don't care about getting prayers right. I was a slip-out-of-the-back-at-communion Catholic, and I was the same kind of Jew. No matter what religion I'm in, I do not do a deep dive into the religious part. I am all about the social and social activist part. So I loved making costumes for the Purim spiel play, a comic play that is part of the holiday of Purim. I organized food kitchens for Hebrew school kids. I drove them to Jewish cemeteries to pull weeds. And, I was instrumental in my synagogue's effort to help refugees and connected my synagogue with Rutgers for an ongoing and fruitful partnership that continues to this day. There are many ways of practicing religion and mine is social justice action.

Interpreting the Torah? Not for me. Accurate pronunciation of Hebrew prayers? I am just not putting my time into that. But that was just the start of my ex-husband's criticism of me as a Jew. He was most critical about the way I handled our children's religious educations. As our marriage ended, he told me he had always feared they would not grow up to be Jews. And if they did not, he said it would be my fault.

Belief was as important to him as it was to any evangelical, it seemed to me. And, of course, he made me the consummate Eve, leading our kids astray.

I'm not going to discuss my kids' faith here. It's their story to tell, if they ever want to, not mine.

Here's the end of my religious story. I don't go to synagogue. The beautiful sanctuary I had once so admired makes my heart thump and not from joy. The songs and prayers I had so earnestly learned shoot my blood pressure up. When I listened to Ruth Bader Ginsberg's funeral service, I had to turn down the music. Hearing it put me back into a dark place I thought I had escaped. Once I recognized and accepted the fact that we were going to get divorced, I felt as though I had just crawled out of a smoking pit of despair. I felt that I had pulled myself out of that hole, stood up, brushed ash and dirt off myself and begun a long walk back toward the world I came from, a world of light. And it was a hard walk. Sometimes I could feel glowing coals come shooting out of that pit toward me and I tried to neutralize them with love. Even today I sometimes feel tentacles inching out of that hole, reaching out for my ankles. Some of it was stuff he actually did. But some of it is his voice and the awful way it made me feel echoing in my head. I can do something about that. I am making progress on rewiring my brain and squeezing him and that old misery out of it. Sadly, the sounds of Jewish prayers are interwoven with his voice and the pain it caused me. I can't untangle the two. And now that I've escaped those dark depths and have pushed so much of them out of my brain, there is no way I'm going near anything that threatens to suck me back into that terrible vortex.

I am wary of religion; I've seen it weaponized in our nation and in my life. But, I do trust religious people who are honest about loving God and loving their fellow humans. I can see how their faith supports them as they help people right here on earth. I respect that.

When I visit my mother, I go to Catholic church with her. It's at a chapel on a military base. I love the priests who officiate at services there. I went to one of them for solace and advice when my marriage ended. I didn't go to him because he was a priest. I went to him because he was a wise man. I knew that it was good that my marriage was ending. But it also tore me apart. I had invested so much in this relationship. It wasn't just that the guy broke my heart. Without my realizing it, being a wife had become my identity. When your world and what you think you are disintegrate, even when a lot of it was a fantasy you had spun in your own head, it is really, really hard to let go of that illusion.

So, while home in Wisconsin when it seemed that a lot of my world and my role in it had shattered, I went to see my mother's priest.

"He's a priest," said one of my brothers, who is a weekly churchgoer, just as my dad was. "He's going to try to talk you into staying married."

He did not.

I poured out my story to him. He just listened.

The very first thing he said was that God loves me.

"You know how much you love your children? God loves you even more."

Wow. That was a great thing to hear.

He didn't say a thing about belief. He asked me about my marriage. Then he talked about new doors opening when old ones closed. He said that my marriage would always be with me, but that I would be able to move on.

He told me that there was more to life than I had been getting and that I would get it.

My rabbis at my synagogue always described God as a being of love and kindness. But, since their voices were intertwined with my ex-husband's — through no fault of theirs — I couldn't bear to go to them.

Although I am not religious, I respect those who are truly religious and whose communing with God helps them deal wisely with people right here on earth. Just like with my dad.

That is why the hypocrisy of the way the far right co-opted God so infuriated me that I flirted with calling this book, *Not All Christians Are Pricks*.

Proving that not all Christians are pricks turned into a quest for me, as an individual and as an American. A nation that guarantees freedom of religion also guarantees freedom from religion. It means no one can force his or her religion upon you. Once religion isn't running the show, the secular and the unaffiliated are comfortable working with the religious because they are not afraid of being preached at. Or shamed.

Keeping religion out of politics is more important than ever. We're in dangerous times right now. Really dangerous. A Republican Party hijacked by the right, which used religion to build its power, threatens our democracy. This is not partisan battle of Republicans vs. Democrats, to quote Stacey Abrams. This is the Republican Party against democracy.

Saving our democracy means we have to work as hard as we possibly can to find like-minded people. We'll find them in churches and outside of churches. We have to look beyond labels — progressive, liberal, conservative, Democrat, Republican — and to the issues. We have to reframe the conversation.

Reproductive choice, for example, is not just about abortion.

It's about keeping contraception legal. The Catholic Church was the first church to condemn abortion. It also — and always has — forbids any "artificial" use of birth control. That means not just oral contraceptives and IUDs (which, because they prevent fertilized eggs from attaching to walls of the uterus, are what the church calls abortifacient), it means condoms and diaphragms. Pope Francis seems to be more lenient on some of this but he's the head of a big ship that's going to be tough to turn around. And a lot of the crew he commands, especially American bishops, are mutinous.

So we have to work the margins, reframe the conversations, look beyond labels — religious or political — and instead, talk good jobs, clean air, clean water, voter rights and equality for all.

I believe in me. I believe in you. Let's get to work.

Keep the faith.

ABOUT THE AUTHOR

Kate Rice is a runner, ex-ski bum, java junkie, loyal Green Bay Packer fan and a rock'n roll singer and stand up comic who performs mostly in the shower but sometimes on stage.

She is a prizewinning reporter and an activist who believes that to be a citizen of this great country is both a gift and a responsibility.

 twitter.com/katericeviews
 instagram.com/katericeviews

ALSO BY KATE RICE

How Refugee Resettlement Unites America: Where Right, Left and Center Work Together

Made in the USA
Middletown, DE
13 October 2021